AMAZING
POWER
OF
FAITH

By

Merlin R. Carothers

AMAZING POWER OF FAITH

ISBN10: 0-940326-45-8

ISBN13: 978-0943026-45-9

www.merlincarothers.com

Unless otherwise noted, Scripture quotations are taken from The Living Bible,

© 1971. Used with permission by Tyndale House Publisher, Inc. Wheaton, Illinois.

Additional Books
by
Merlin Carothers

Prison to Praise
Power in Praise
Answers to Praise
Praise Works!
Walking & Leaping
Bringing Heaven into Hell
Victory on Praise Mountain
The Bible on Praise
More Power to You
What's on Your Mind?
Let Me Entertain You
From Fear to Faith
You Can Be Happy Now
Secret Sins
God's Secret Weapon

ACKNOWLEDGEMENTS

I am thankful for the loving encouragement to write this book given by our daughter, Joann Thomas and our staff members, Sally Huffman and Janie Malkovic, and the editing help of our talented friend, Hope Welsh.

INTRODUCTION

There are many things we *hope* will happen, but *hoping* and *knowing* are quite different.

Jesus told His disciples many things that they could do if they had more faith.

They learned!

They recorded what they learned.

I pray that each page of this book will help you to understand what they learned.

MY LAST BOOK

After I finished my last book, I asked the Lord if it was okay with Him for me to lay down my pen and rest. He didn't give me an answer. A short time later while I was taking a leisurely stroll in our beautiful community, a thought came to me: "Is there anything especially important that you believe everyone needs to know?"

I thought about the many letters I receive each day from hurting people. What did they need?

Soon I knew the answer to the question. They needed to have more faith. But how could I help them?

I thought, prayed, and sought God's guidance. I confess that I told Him I was tired. Not because I was 87, but because of what I had done during those years. I hadn't done as much as some people, but after four wars and multiple injuries, I felt exhausted.

After writing, publishing and distributing fifteen books it seemed to me that I had written everything I knew.

No pressure, son. Do what you think is best.

So I began studying what the Bible says about having faith in God. I was surprised at the multitude of things that became clearer to me. My energy and zeal increased.

Throughout the Old and New Testament one of the messages is clear. Whenever men and women had faith in what God would do for them, amazing things happened.

Many people do not know about God's most important gift. The more I thought about it, the more I realized what God wanted me to share with you.

Each one of us needs to know and to understand the miracle that Jesus came to offer us.

Please read portions of this devotional every day. Listen to what God is saying to *you*. I hope you will learn as much as I did as I wrote the following pages.

ALMOST TOO GOOD TO BELIEVE

God sent Jesus to do something so wonderful that many people are unable to believe it. Just think of it: God sent His own Son to pay the penalty for every one of our sins! What a gift! Why did He do this?

God made me His adopted son. What benefits does that give me? The more I searched through Scripture on this subject the more enthusiastic I became.

I wrote page after page of Scripture verses

that clearly explain the gifts He offers us. As I studied, the Holy Spirit kept lifting my spirit in new joy over what God has done. I was learning more of what it means to be God's son.

Think of the many times you have prayed what Jesus taught us to pray, "Our Father who art in Heaven." If He is your father, what does that make you? You must be *His child* for Him to be *your Father*.

If my father, Dave Carothers, were the President of the United States, I know that I, Merlin, would have certain benefits. I could go to the front gate of the White House and the guards would know me. They would know they should get me to the President as quickly as possible because that was the written order of the President. No other official in the entire government would get the quick, full service that I would receive. Why? Did I do something wonderful? No. The guards would be interested in only one thing: the President's order.

What an illustration that is to me! I am God's son! He loves to talk to me anytime I want to be with Him. He wants to do for me anything that He knows will help me. I am like the Prodigal Son who returned to his father. The son thought he was not worthy to even be his father's servant. That's the way I used to feel about God. I thought I wasn't worthy.

I didn't have absolute faith that I would be with Him forever as one of His children. I had been so disobedient, and would probably do even more that would displease Him! How could I be absolutely positive that He would take me to Heaven? Now I understand the *Miracle of Faith.*

Now I know who I am! I know, without a doubt, that I am not worthy of such an exalted honor, but God has decided that He wants to give honor to His children. Not because of whom the child is but because of who He is. I want you to have that honor, know that you have it, and revel in it. Then you will be free to tell everyone who you are, and how they too can be one of God's beloved children.

ARE YOU SURE OR UNSURE?

Will you go to Heaven? Are you sure? Are you unsure?

If you are sometimes unsure what will happen when you die, read these daily devotions until they become so real to you that you can help other people to know what you know. We need to know what we know! The Holy Spirit will create in you a spirit of joy that will gradually become a *feeling of victory.*

I have been at the bedside of hundreds of men and women when they believed they would soon die. Every one of them wanted to know what would happen the moment they died.

The Apostle Paul was chained in a prison cell – year after year – and it was there that he wrote about his joy. When Jesus lives in us He wants to give us the same assurance that Paul had!

Now glory be to God who by his mighty power at work within us is able to do far more than we would ever dare to ask or even dream of – infinitely beyond our highest prayers, desires, thoughts, or hopes. (Ephesians 3:20)

He does the working. We do the believing.

If Jesus lives in us, we are sure we are going to Heaven. When anyone is sure, it changes – everything. We know what we know!

How many people are absolutely sure they are going to Heaven? Many hope they will but by their own words admit they are not sure.

An increasing number of people believe that many religions can lead us to Heaven. But Jesus said:

I am the way and the truth and the life. No one comes to the Father except through Me. (John 14:6 NIV)

Was Jesus right or wrong?

Back in the 16th Century it was illegal for anyone, except priests, to have a Bible. But one man, Martin Luther, risked his life by declaring that everyone should have a Bible.

The Protestant faith was born.

Now, you and I can help many people who do not know what the Bible says, to know that because of Jesus anyone can be sure they are a child of God.

WHO WILL GO TO HEAVEN?

Some people believe that if they try to be a good person they will go to Heaven.

Others believe that if they try to be a good person and go to church regularly they will go to Heaven.

But we do not decide what we must do. God decides. He knows that the heart of man is desperately wicked:

The heart is the most deceitful thing there is, and desperately wicked. No one can really know how bad it is! (Jeremiah 17:9)

What might we do if caught in a situation where it seemed like the only solution was to do something "evil"? God knows what we might do!

Eternal life with God is a very important part of His plan. Because He is perfectly holy there is only one way He can admit us into Heaven. We have to be perfectly pure and righteous. But we can only have that perfection through Jesus, His Son. Living a good life will never be good enough because no one can be perfect. But Jesus' perfect righteousness can be ours!

Only those who believe in Jesus *as their Savior* will enter Heaven. God made that point clear in hundreds of Bible verses. Do you know what they say? I strongly recommend that you need to know! In this book you will learn many of them.

Know what you believe. Satan will temp you, over and over, to wonder if you know for sure that God has written your name in His Book of Eternal Life. He tempts us to disbelieve everything that God says! Learn everything you can about everything He says He wants to do for us.

KNOWING GOD'S LOVE

Over the past 60 years I have read hundreds of Christian books. Many of them blessed and encouraged me. Now this book is blessing me! It contains material that will lead many people into knowing, really knowing, that they are going to Heaven!

If you already believe that you are saved by faith in Jesus, this book is not an attempt to change what you believe. Rather, it is designed to help you practice what you believe. For example, if someone asks if you are a Christian do not hesitate to answer,

"Yes, I know that I am." This is the answer that will please God. You are not honoring yourself but His Son!

Life convinces most of us that loving and being loved are the most important elements of happiness! But imagine children who believe that their parents do not love them.

God created us to love and be loved. We demonstrate this by the way we react when we feel unloved. *God is love* and He wants our love more than anything we could do or accomplish for Him. I exhort you to make this your primary goal.

No service to God is as important to Him as our efforts to convince others that He wants to give us His *free gift of eternal life.*

Satan does not want us to believe that God loves us. He whispers, "If God were good and all-powerful He would stop the evil that happens all around you." But it is evil that creates pain, hardship and unhappiness.

Do you have the joy of knowing that someone loves you more than they love themselves? Please receive the joy of knowing that God loves you so much that He is willing to give you the perfection that Jesus had while He lived here on earth! He gives this gift because that is what He promised to do for anyone who would believe Him. *We know how much God loves us because we have felt his love and because we believe him when he tells us that he loves us dearly. God is love, and anyone who lives in love is living with God and God is living in him.* (1 John 4:16)

Being certain that God loves us satisfies the need He placed in us!

FILLED WITH JOY

I have told you this so that you will be filled with my joy. Yes, your cup of joy will overflow! (John 15:11)

Filled with joy? Joy that overflows? Jesus' disciples must have wondered how He could fulfill that promise.

Jesus knew that his disciples would be filled with joy. But they couldn't comprehend how they could be happy if He left them. Their faith was weak and they knew it. Later they learned to believe what Jesus had told them. You and I can learn.

In this book I am emphasizing that by your faith you can be filled with miraculous joy. Are you skeptical about what I'm saying because I know nothing about your problems?

I know that when I believed Jesus' promise, my own joy made a giant leap forward. The stronger my faith becomes the more I experience His joy. Many people tell me that they are having the same experience.

Some folks take longer to know their joy is

increasing, but God gives a solution. He says:

And let us not get tired of doing what is right, for after a while we will reap a harvest of blessing if we don't give up. (Galatians 6:9)

Some of us are harder to convince than others. But when we become convinced that our joy can be full and overflowing we become God's messengers to others who are also hard to convince! Jesus and His Holy Spirit are here to help us receive the "impossible."

If you lack wisdom in how to accomplish such great things God gives us the solution:

If you want to know what God wants you to do, ask him, and he will gladly tell you, for he is always ready to give a bountiful supply of wisdom to all who ask him; he will not resent it. (James 1:5)

Jesus told us to:

Keep on asking and you will keep on getting; keep on looking and you will keep on finding. (Luke 11:9)

Reading these pages means that you are "looking." *"Keep on looking and you will keep on finding."*

If you lack wisdom, ask God and He will give you whatever you need to be what He wants you to be. There is nothing more glorious than being what He wants us to be!

ONLY BY FAITH

A young man fell in love with a beautiful young lady. It seemed to him that every time he saw her he learned something new about her, and he marveled that one girl should be everything he had ever hoped to find. She was so-o-o attractive. He had never imagined that there could be such a divine creature.

The young man was in the same college class as this "angel." He saw her every day and often managed to sit near her. When he spoke to her, she responded politely but seemed disinterested in carrying on a conversation with him. His heart was nearly broken as he observed and overheard her cheerful conversations with other young men. At many school functions he saw her being escorted by different men and he felt uncontrollably jealous. They held her hand and sat close to her. He would feel his heart beating rapidly and he had a feeling of hopelessness.

Over and over this sad young man rehearsed the invitation he would give the young lady to go on a date with him. But when he saw her look at him without seeing him, he would flee and try to compose another invitation.

One day his darkness turned to day. He came face to face with her in a school hallway and before he could think of what he would say, he said, "Could I take you to dinner next Saturday evening?" She smiled and said, "Yes."

The lovesick young man floated away. She had said yes! For the rest of the week he planned how he would make this the best date the young lady had ever had: flowers, reservation at the best restaurant, and the best table. He spoke to the waiter who would serve them and explained how important the evening would be. He promised the waiter an unusually high tip if he made the young lady feel very special.

The young man purchased a new suit, shirt, tie, and special shoes. His father said, "Yes, you may use the family car that night." So he washed and polished the car. When his father saw how excited his son was, he told him how pleased he was to see him so happy.

Finally Saturday night arrived. At the agreed time he arrived at the girl's home. Her mother answered the doorbell and seemed surprised to see this elegantly dressed young man standing there with a beautiful bouquet. "Can I help you?" she asked.

"Yes, I'm here to pick up your daughter," the young man said. "We are going out for dinner." The mother seemed even more surprised.

"Just a minute," she said, "I'll tell her you're here. What is your name?"

After few agonizing minutes the beautiful

"angel" appeared. "Hello," she said in a questioning way. "Mother says you came to take me out. Why did you think we had a date?"

The young man lost his tongue and stammered, "You told me you would go to dinner with me tonight."

"I thought you were kidding," she said. "I'm not ready to go anywhere. I'm sorry I misunderstood you."

With that the young man turned and left. And he let himself believe that he had no hope of ever being accepted by his "angel".

Yes, it's just a story, but I've seen it played out in the lives of so many people. Jesus invited them to go with Him and to live with Him in Heaven for eternity. They say, "Yes I want to."

Then someone asks them if they are going to Heaven and they respond with, "I don't know." With just a few words they are saying that they don't believe what Jesus told us. They confess that they are not sure what He said. When they pray they do not think of beginning with, "Hello Father. This is your child."

The above illustration isn't perfect but the comparison is real. We must know for sure what Jesus tells us and know exactly what we believe.

REPETITION

As you read, you may eventually feel like I'm going over and over the same subjects. I have good reasons for doing so. From our first grade in school we learned by repetition. We may hear something once, even understand it, but then forget what we learned. I have heard from thousands of people who don't remember what Jesus has done for them. They keep concentrating on ways to solve the problems that Jesus has already solved for them.

Jesus knew and practiced the perfect solutions. When faced with a problem He didn't have to seek for a solution. He was the solution.

The disciples had no food to feed the multitude. Jesus multiplied the tiny bit they had. Then the storm was nearly sinking their boat. No problem: Jesus told the storm to be quiet and it was quiet.

You may be thinking, "But I can't do any of those things." Jesus wanted his disciples to know that they didn't have to do anything because they could trust Him. He kept teaching His disciples not to worry about storms, money, people – or anything. Eventually they learned. They wrote down what they learned and their discoveries are recorded in the New Testament. Over and over they learned to have faith in God. Now we need to learn what they learned.

No matter how small your faith is, is it growing? Or is life and Satan's temptations pulling you downward? This book is a lifeline between you and God's loving care for you. He wants to take perfect care of you, now and forever.

Are you ready to increase your faith? If so, leap out on the stormy waters and let Jesus pick you up. He will!

THERE ARE NO 'IFS'

A father brought his severely ill child to Jesus and said:

"If You can do anything, do it. Have a heart and help us!"

Jesus said, "If? There are no 'ifs' among believers. Anything can happen."

No sooner were the words out of his mouth than the father cried, "Then I believe. Help me with my doubts!" (Mark 9:22-24 MSG)

Jesus took the boy's hand, raised him up, and he was completely well. The lesson to us is, if you believe, God will make it true. If you believe that Jesus is your Savior, He is your Savior. Note that He did not say, "I am your Savior if you hope that I am."

Jesus responded with power when people

had faith in what He could do for them. A woman had a blood disease for 12 years. She believed that if she touched Him she would be healed. When Jesus saw her He said:

"Daughter . . . all is well! Your faith has healed you." And the woman was well from that moment. (Matthew 9:22)

A synagogue ruler bowed before Jesus and demonstrated an unusual faith. He told Jesus that his daughter had just died but he believed that if Jesus touched her dead body, she would come back to life.

When Jesus arrived at the ruler's home He saw the crowd and heard their traditional weeping over the ruler's loss. Jesus told them that the girl was not dead. They laughed at Him for having such a ridiculous idea.

Jesus took the dead girl's hand and she rose up alive.

Later on two blind men shouted their plea for Jesus to heal them. He asked them if they believed He could. When they said "yes," He healed them. Over and over the Bible repeats the same message:

Because of your faith it will happen. (Matthew 9:29)

For Jesus to be our Savior we must believe that He is our Savior!

Say it: "Jesus, I believe You are my Savior." Say it any time you are tempted to doubt His promise.

GOD'S ONLY REQUIREMENT

For this wonderful news – the message that God wants to save us has been given to us just as it was to those who lived in the time of Moses. But it didn't do them any good because they didn't believe it. They didn't mix it with faith. (Hebrews 4:2)

If we hear but do not understand God's promise of salvation by faith in Jesus, we face the same response from God as those who lived in the time of Moses. What we hear will do us no good if we do not believe it. It seems strange to some people that God would place such a huge importance on what we believe. They may honestly think that actions are more important than what they believe. But God has set His standard and we would be very unwise to disregard what He says.

Consider the fact that God created everything in all creation just by speaking. He's so powerful that he spoke man into existence! Jesus repeatedly showed His power by doing "impossible" things. He could not understand men's lack of faith. God does not excuse our lack of faith in His Son, so we would be wise to spend much of our time in learning to believe Him:

For only we who believe God can enter into his place of rest. He has said, "I have sworn in my anger that those who don't believe me will never get in." (Hebrews 4:3)

We will only enter into God's place of rest if we believe Him.

This includes you who were once so far away from God. You were his enemies and hated him and were separated from him by your evil thoughts and actions, yet now he has brought you back as his friends. He has done this through the death on the cross of his own human body, and now as a result Christ has brought you into the very presence of God, and you are standing there before him with nothing left against you –nothing left that he could even chide you for; the only condition is that you fully believe the Truth, standing in it steadfast and firm, strong in the Lord, convinced of the Good News that Jesus died for you, and never shifting from trusting him to save you. This is the wonderful news that came to each of you and is now spreading all over the world. And I, Paul, have the joy of telling it to others. (Colossians 1:21-23)

God's only requirement is that we believe the truth!

You were dead in sins, and your sinful desires were not yet cut away. Then he gave you a share in the very life of Christ. (Colossians 2:13)

Know that God blotted out the charges against you, and the commandments that you had not obeyed. He takes this list of sins and destroys them by nailing them to Christ's cross:

For he forgave all your sins, and blotted out the charges proved against you, the list of his commandments which you had not obeyed. He took this list of sins and destroyed it by nailing it to Christ's cross. (Colossians 2:13-14)

And now Jesus is able to present you to God as holy in His sight, without blemish and free from all accusations against you!

UP TO THE END

When Jesus returns will we cringe in fear as we remember the things we did wrong and the things we could have done better? Read what the Bible tells us. Study this promise:

Now you have every grace and blessing; every spiritual gift and power for doing his will are yours during this time of waiting for the return of our Lord Jesus Christ. And he guarantees right up to the end that you will be counted free from all sin and guilt on that day when he returns. (1 Corinthians 1:7-8)

He guarantees! He doesn't say we will never sin again. He knows we are not capable of never sinning again. But, *right up to the end* we will be free from all sin and guilt!

Paul was writing to ordinary people like you and me. We should focus on the wonderful gifts God has given us.

Only Jesus has the power to do anything about our sins:

All praise to him who always loves us and who set us free from our sins by pouring out his lifeblood for us. (Revelation 1:5)

Yes, God will reward us in Heaven for the work we have done for Him, but entry into Heaven has already been promised to those who trust in Jesus as Savior.

So, my dear brothers, since future victory is sure, be strong and steady, always abounding in the Lord's work, for you know that nothing you do for the Lord is ever wasted. (1 Corinthians 15:58)

The more I understand the greatness of God's love, the stronger my desire to love and serve Him grows.

BUILDING OUR FAITH

If we want to have money in the bank to help us when we are old, we need to save money while we can. Sounds sensible but many folks are never quite ready to do so.

Likewise if we want to have faith when we need God's help, we need to learn how to build our faith. We can do this!

Here is a simple example. I used to grumble when I was tired and wanted to go to bed but still needed to brush my teeth. Because of persistently sore gums I needed to brush and then use even smaller brushes to get between my teeth. It seemed to me to take forever. But then it dawned on me that I had not learned to be thankful that I could still do that simple task. When I was young I seldom had a toothbrush! Even when I did, more often than not I did not have toothpaste.

So I started being thankful that I now I have two or more of each.

Many times I think of new a reason to be happy, such as being able to walk. Often my feet want to complain, so I think of how marvelous it is that I can still walk! For many years I had no mode of transportation so I had to walk no matter how far it was.

My list goes on and on but you see my point. God wants us to learn how to be thankful for *whatever we have.* If we wait too long it will become harder and harder to learn.

Are you building your faith? Keep reading!

LOVING GOD

Jesus said the most important thing for us to do is to love God with all our heart, soul, mind and strength. We must try to keep that commandment! You know that you cannot force yourself to love God, so what can you do to obey Jesus' command?

I want to share with you, as simply and as clearly as I can how we can learn to do what Jesus tells us to do. The more clearly you understand and follow the command Jesus gave us, the happier you will be. Then you will want everyone to know what you have learned! And Christ's plan will seem so simple that you will wonder why you had never understood it.

God wants to deliver us from the sin nature we had when we were born. We want to do bad things, even though at times we want to do good things. Sometimes the bad in us overcomes the good. But God provides a way for us to be forgiven. He gives us the free gift of His own love that He demonstrated through Jesus.

God designed His Good News so carefully that we can teach even little children to understand it!

Jesus pointed us toward little children. They can joyfully sing, "Jesus loves the little children, all the children of the world," and they usually believe what they're singing. The problems of life have not yet convinced them that God doesn't love them. But you and I need help.

God wants to help us in our unbelief. He wants to do this so much that He gave His only Son to help us. Once we understand His forgiveness, the more we fall in love with Him! Loving God becomes the center of our lives!

And I pray that Christ will be more and more at home in your hearts, living within you as you trust in him. May your roots go down deep into the soil of God's marvelous love; and may you be able to feel and understand, as all God's children should, how long, how wide, how deep, and how high his love really is; and to experience this love for yourselves, though it is so great that you will never see the end of it or fully know or understand it. And so at last you will be filled up with God himself. (Ephesians 3:17-19)

Jesus' enemies had Him arrested. Then Peter cursed and swore that he had never known Him. The result? Jesus forgave Him. Peter spent the rest of his life urging people to trust Jesus to forgive all their sins and failures. God caused Peter's horrible failure to work for good!

OUR PROBLEM SOLVER

When Jesus was here on earth He solved problems of many kinds. When food was needed He supplied it. When people were sick He made them well. When people died He raised them from the dead. When fishermen could find no fish He found fish for them.

When a storm was about to sink their boat He told the storm to be quiet. When His disciples needed money He told them where they could find it.

What a life people enjoyed when Jesus was close to them! He answered any questions they had. A woman accused of adultery? He had a perfect answer. Moral, legal or political questions posed no problem for Him.

What about today? He's given us His perfect solution:

I am with you always, even to the end of the world. (Matthew 28:20)

Perfect solution? Yes! Sufficient to cause His power to work in us in every situation.

We can decide when and where we will drive our automobile. We can trust Him to guide us. But what about other drivers? Therein lays our power. Jesus can guide us where to drive and when, but He can also control other drivers just as He controlled the storms that threatened His disciples! We can decide to ride in an airplane but we have no control over the pilot or the many people who service the plane. But Jesus has total control over them! We can order our food in a restaurant and have no control over when it will be served. But God can control the restaurant and everyone who works there. So we have no reason to be upset over what others do or don't do.

When we go to church we may have no control over what happens but we can believe that God will bless us by whatever is done. He can cause the music, the hymns, the sermon, and everything to bless us. We have no reason to be critical or concerned about anything. What joy and power it gives us when we know that Jesus rules and reigns!

Problems come to us by the dozens. How are we to solve them? Jesus wants us to trust Him, every minute of every day. Will that work?

Jesus touched the blind and immediately they could see.

When a man who could not speak was brought to Him, Jesus healed him.

And so went just part of one day with Jesus. Would you like to have been there to watch? But not one of those miracles can compare to what happens when we believe in Jesus as our Savior!

PLEASE WASH MY FEET

Jesus knelt before Peter and wanted to wash his feet. Only the lowest servant would perform that menial task. Peter told Jesus that He would never permit Him to do such a thing to him. Peter's response is similar to that made by people when they are told that they must believe Jesus forgives all their sins. They think they should be a better person and should not expect Jesus to wash away their sins.

Imagine Peter's surprise when Jesus told him:

If I do not wash you, you have no part with Me. (John 13:8 NASB)

Peter understood and said to Him:

Then wash my hands and head as well – not just my feet! (John 13:9)

We must believe that we will enter Heaven only by receiving Jesus' *free gift*. Once we receive that gift we want to share with others what He will do for them.

Do you understand that when we stand before God it will do us no good to tell Him how difficult it was for us to obey Him? He knows all about our weakness. He wants us to place our trust and hope in His Son.

Our best plan is to accept God's plan!

FACING IMPOSSIBLE OBSTACLES

The Philistine giant, Goliath, challenged the Israelites to send a man to fight him.

Goliath was 13 feet tall. David was a young shepherd boy. But there was another difference. Goliath trusted in himself. David trusted in God.

All the Philistines, and even the Israelites, thought David had no chance to defeat such a giant. David was not concerned about either opinion. He wanted to bring glory to God.

David picked up a small stone, placed it in his slingshot and ran toward the giant. His tiny stone hit the giant's head, the giant fell down, and David cut his head off: end of battle.

The Philistines saw what happened and were in such a panic that they headed for home as fast as they could go, with the Israelites in full pursuit.

Why is this story in the Bible? What was God's intent? You and I can consider this event thousands of years later and realize that we can defeat Satan. Satan doesn't want us to have faith in God. He is not afraid of us, but he will flee when he sees our faith in the One who defeated him at Calvary.

God uses our faith to win battles.

Are you afraid that your faith is too weak for you to be certain that you are going to Heaven? Pick up your weapon: God's promises. They are quoted throughout this book. God will bless even pebble-sized faith to defeat the giant of unbelief.

WHAT GOD HAS PROMISED?

We may face school, work, marriage, children and unending challenges as we try to make it from day to day. We rarely take time to consider what God has promised:

Great peace of heart and mind. (1 Corinthians 1:3)

Paul understood the need for this peace so he repeatedly wrote about the gifts that God has given us:

And He guarantees right up to the end that you will be counted free from all sin and guilt on that day when he returns. (1 Corinthians 1:8)

Right up to the end of your life God is willing to count you as free from all sins and guilt if you believe that Jesus gave Himself to purchase your salvation. Sound too easy? Remember the price Jesus paid in order that we might have this free gift.

From his own life Paul knew that we are all tempted to doubt God's free gift. He wrote:

For it is from God alone that you have your life through Christ Jesus. He showed us God's plan of salvation; he was the one who made us acceptable to God; he made us pure and holy and gave himself to purchase our salvation. (1 Corinthians 1:30)

Note that Jesus made us acceptable to God. *We could never make or even keep ourselves acceptable.* That is why God sacrificed His only Son. He wanted to help us do what we could never do for ourselves! We could never make ourselves pure and holy. We could not purchase our own salvation to make ourselves acceptable to God.

And again Paul wrote:

Now your sins are washed away, and you are set apart for God, and he has accepted you because of what the Lord Jesus Christ and the Spirit of our God have done for you. (1 Corinthians 6:11)

Please take your pen or pencil and circle that verse. Refer to it when Satan whispers, "You are not good enough." Smile and say, "I know that."

Jesus said that we must seek His help in order to receive His help:

Jesus shouted to the crowds, "If anyone is thirsty, let him come to me and drink." (John 7:37)

He will satisfy our thirst.

Are you thirsty? Do you need peace? Take time to consider what God has promised us in His Word.

GOD'S KINDNESS

Throughout the Old Testament God's people refused to obey Him. They always had what they considered to be a good reason, but God did not accept their excuses.

We still have a strong tendency to be disobedient today, so God bases our salvation on our faith in Jesus. Yet sometimes we try to base our confidence on what we are and what we do. When we do this we face the same results as the Israelites. They were forced to wander in the wilderness for forty years. Not an easy way to learn!

It is better if we learn to believe we are saved by God's kindness:

If they are saved by God's kindness, then it is not by their good works. For in that case, God's wonderful kindness would not be what it really is - free and undeserved. (Romans 11:6)

God's wonderful kindness toward us is free and undeserved. When we believe that, it changes the way we live.

When we have faith in God's goodness toward us we have an increasing desire not to sin.

That's what happens when we trust in Jesus: *we experience an increasing desire not to sin.* What a miracle! Once we experience that blessing we begin to understand that God desires to help us, not condemn us!

Paul emphasized this blessing when he wrote:

Then you will learn from your own expe-

rience how his ways will really satisfy you. (Romans 12:2)

God not only saves us by His kindness, He satisfies us by His kindness. Paul goes on to explain that we experience this blessing when we believe God:

God who gives you hope will keep you happy and full of peace as you believe in him. I pray that God will help you overflow with hope in him through the Holy Spirit's power within you. (Romans 15:13)

LEARNING TO INCREASE OUR FAITH

How can we increase our faith? The answer is not a secret that has to be revealed to us by a miracle. Jesus' disciples saw many miracles and they were still unable to have the faith that Jesus said they should have. He said to them:

Oh, you stubborn, faithless people! How long shall I bear with you? (Matthew 17:17)

We need to grow in faith! We can grow NOW! We can learn to believe in the promises that God gave us.

When Jesus spoke sternly to people about their lack of faith, He knew they could believe Him if they would open their eyes and try to believe.

We can spend a lifetime believing only what

we can see or feel. Or we can increase our faith by placing our attention on, and doing, what Jesus told us to do. He told us that the Holy Spirit would lead us into all truth. We can learn to be led but too often we want to learn what we want to learn.

ADAM AND EVE

Adam and Eve walked and talked with God. They could ask Him anything they wanted to know. They didn't ask Him why they had sickness or pain because they never experienced suffering!

We do not know how long Adam and Eve lived before they sinned. Perhaps even hundreds of years. God had created them with no potential to grow old.

But God had given them free will. They could do whatever they wanted to do. This gave them the liberty to break the one law He had given them: they must not eat the fruit of one tree in the garden.

Satan had once lived with God. He too had the potential to live under God's blessing. He had a powerful position in Heaven but he wanted more power, so he rebelled and convinced many angels to follow him. He jealously watched Adam and Eve and plotted ways to destroy them.

Then Satan found an opportunity to convince Eve to enjoy the forbidden fruit. Do this, he said, and you will become like God. She ate, enjoyed, and convinced Adam to eat with her. They became separated from God, just as we are before we learn to trust in Jesus as our Savior.

If you think of yourself as a fairly good person, do you still have the potential to make bad decisions like Adam and Eve did? They were perfect but they had the potential to do what God told them they must not do.

We all have the same potential to do something that God has said we should not do. If you hope for Heaven because you are a fairly good person, think again!

Jesus came to give us something we could not possibly attain for ourselves. We need God to do something *for us*. He did that when He sent His Son to die for us! He tells us very clearly that the only way we can enter Heaven is by believing that He gives us a free gift:

Because of his kindness you have been saved through trusting Christ. And even trusting is not of yourselves; it too is a gift from God. Salvation is not a reward for the good we have done, so none of us can take any credit for it. (Ephesians 2:8-9)

None of us can take any credit! Remember – none of us.

Once we receive God's free gift, we strive

to be obedient to Him. But we are never good enough to enter Heaven by our own perfection.

Please remember that the only way any person will ever enter Heaven is to be perfect. Only the righteousness of Jesus will qualify someone to enter the place He has prepared for eternity.

We do have one great opportunity to do something for ourselves:

But store up for yourselves treasures in heaven. (Matthew 6:20 NIV)

BE STRONG

"Be strong in the Lord." You may have heard that phrase before. There are things we can accomplish that are way beyond our natural ability. Your faith in Him can release powers in you to do the "impossible." My own life is a living example of His might working in me to do things I could not possibly have done on my own.

Some folks have tried to test God rather than permit Him to test them! For example, they have tried to pick up a 300-pound weight to see if He would help them do so. We should first believe that He would help us do whatever He wants us to do. You can decide right now that you will do whatever He wants you to do.

If you fail today, try again tomorrow.

I knew I could never be a preacher. I didn't have the needed speaking ability. My college teachers agreed with me. They recommended that I prepare for another way to serve the Lord. I didn't have the needed skills to be a writer. Once again, my teachers agreed. But we did not understand what God can do if we believe what He says:

I can do everything God asks me to with the help of Christ who gives me the strength and power. (Philippians 4:13)

Does that promise sound too simplistic to fit your situation? I once felt the same way, but I learned that God always keeps His promises when we believe Him.

TURN THE KEY

"The true Bread is a Person – the one sent by God from heaven, and he gives life to the world."

"Sir," they said, "give us that bread every day of our lives!"

Jesus replied, "I am the Bread of Life. No one coming to me will ever be hungry again. Those believing in me will never thirst." (John 6:33-35)

For thousands of years men considered bread to be their essential means of staying alive. People were hungry when they had no bread. When Jesus said He could help them never to be hungry again, He had their attention.

We have an abundance of food today and are less inclined to understand what Jesus meant. He will supply whatever we need, if we believe. We need to believe Him whenever we desperately need His help.

The people asked Jesus to give them bread every day.

Jesus' response indicates that He wanted to give them not just bread, but the bread of life. We are often very like the people Jesus was talking to. We want material things when He wants to give us the true bread of God. If we feast on the life that He gives us we will have exactly what we need.

So His message is, feast on the life that I give you and you will eat your way to Heaven!

AN IMPORTANT EVENT

Reading these pages could be the most important event of your life.

Many people think they understand what God can do, but they are uncertain about what they believe He has done.

If you know and believe God's Good News, this book will help you share your understanding with many people.

God selected Abraham to be an important leader of the Israelites because he had strong faith. That was an early indication of how highly God values our faith:

What's more, the Scriptures looked forward to this time when God would save the gentiles also, through their faith. God told Abraham about this long ago when he said, "I will bless those in every nation who trust in me as you do." And so it is: all who trust in Christ share the same blessing Abraham received. (Galatians 3:8-9)

It is an important event when it dawns on us that we are justified before God by our faith in His Son.

I am reminded of what God told the prophet Jeremiah to tell His people: *The wonderful heritage I reserved for you will slip out of your hand.* (Jeremiah 17:4)

Salvation by faith in Christ can *slip out of our hands* if we fail to believe God's promise!!

TESTIMONY TIME

Many churches once had a testimony time. People would stand up and tell what God had done for them.

In their testimonies people freely reported being born again, their victories, goals, and efforts to share their faith with others.

Testimonies would often be interrupted by joyful shouts of "Praise the Lord!"

This was a period when many Christians were uninhibited about telling others how they knew they were going to Heaven.

Times have changed.

Now the terms "born again" and "saved" are not used in many churches. Not so with Jesus. He said:

With all the earnestness I possess I tell you this: Unless you are born again, you can never get into the Kingdom of God. (John 3:3)

With all the earnestness that I possess I urge you to believe and confess that Jesus has caused you to be born again.

Knowing that we are born again gives us confidence. This new life is as real as our old life! How?

Now your sins are washed away, and you are set apart for God, and he has accepted you because of what the Lord Jesus Christ and the Spirit of our God have done for you. (1 Corinthians 6:11)

For it is from God alone that you have your life through Christ Jesus. He showed us God's plan of salvation; he was the one who made us acceptable to God; he made us pure and holy and gave himself to purchase our salvation. (1 Corinthians 1:30)

Only Jesus can make us acceptable to God!

MOST IMPORTANT DECISION

What is the most important decision you will ever make? Does it have to do with school, work, business, marriage, where to live, finding a home or a church to attend? No!

You may have already made your most important decision. You make your most important decision when you decide what you believe about Jesus. That He was born and lived on earth? No. Or that He was crucified and then resurrected? No.

To receive the gifts that God wants to give us, we must believe that He has given us His free gift of eternal life though Jesus. Once we believe that, He will help us make other decisions.

Even if we make wrong decisions He will make them work for our good!

If you haven't made your most important decision, now is the time! Believe that God gives you His gift of eternal life. Why would He do this for you? Because you are a good person? NO! Because of *who He is*. He was willing to give His life for you. And all you have to do is to have faith that He did what you could never do for yourself:

Because of his kindness you have been saved through trusting Christ. And even trusting is not of yourselves; it too is a gift from God. (Ephesians 2:8)

PERFECT EVIDENCE

What does God want from you more than anything else? Service? A pure life?

One of the religious teachers asked Jesus what the most important commandment is. Jesus answered:

The Lord our God is the one and only God. And you must love him with all your heart and soul and mind and strength. (Mark 12:29-30)

What can we do to learn how to obey this commandment? Learn what God wants *to do for us.*

He will do *anything* to help us. Absolutely anything. But He wants children who choose to believe Him. Adam and Eve chose to disobey and that caused a great disaster. God could force us to do anything, but He wants Heaven to be inhabited by those who choose to trust Him. So He gave us perfect evidence that He loves us.

God gave His only Son as proof of His love for us. In return, He requires that we believe that Jesus came to give eternal life as a free gift to anyone who would believe Him. We need this free gift because we don't always love God and obey Him.

God used many witnesses, in many generations, to tell people that He was displeased with them. What more could He do?

God made it possible for us to be transformed into the likeness of His own Son! Not by anything we could do but by the sacrifice of His own Son. Through Him we can be totally, completely, and absolutely sure we are going to Heaven. He promised to write our names in His Book of Eternal Life.

When we believe what He promised, something happens in us that we could never have achieved on our own. Because of this gift from God we can learn to love Him. We then have joy because this gift is different from any other enjoyment we have known. We know and are positive that we are going to Heaven. God has given us His absolute assurance. What can bring us greater joy? Only one thing I know: we can help others have that same assurance!

MOST IMPORTANT COMMANDMENT

Love the Lord your God with all your heart, soul, and mind. (Matthew 22:37)

For years I wanted to have a better understanding of Jesus' statement. I knew I loved God but wondered if I could look into His eyes and say, "I love You with everything that is in me."

I spent many hours trying to understand why loving God is more important than doing my best to serve Him or living a good life.

As I studied, I was intrigued. One Bible verse led to another. I was so blessed that I kept at it for weeks, and then months.

In the course of my studies I became aware that something new was happening in me. I couldn't explain it but I was beginning to feel differently about God. The more I studied the happier I became. Happier, about what? That's what I wondered.

For many years I had been the happiest person I knew, but I also knew that there was much more that I needed to understand. There are many Bible verses about rejoicing and being glad, but I wasn't reading them during this study. Yet I was simply bubbling with joy. Why?

Satan whispers to us so softly that we may not recognize his voice. Our minds just absorb his lies: "Yes, God is good and He will forgive all your sins if you are good enough." But when we know that we are not good enough to please God we keep wondering how we could learn to be better people.

It kept becoming clearer to me that God does not want us to depend on becoming good enough to get to Heaven. He wants us to do everything we can to be good, obedient children just *because we love Him!*

Nothing we ever do or don't do will be worth anything unless we do it because we love Him.

Even we humans value the small gifts our children give us when we know that they give because they love us!

Please remember: our most important goal is to learn how to love God! My prayer is that as you read this book you will be as inspired as I have been while writing it.

GOD'S GOOD NEWS

For God loved the world so much that he gave his only Son so that anyone who believes in him shall not perish but have eternal life. (John 3:16)

This is the most well-known verse in the Bible.

What does it mean to you?

Does it mean that when we believe in Jesus He gives us everlasting life? Yes, this is His Good News. But what are we to believe about Him? We must believe that God gave Jesus so we could be forgiven for all our sins and have the gift of everlasting life.

God gave His Son for a specific purpose. Please study the above verse to understand why it has helped so many people to receive everlasting life. Now that you've looked at it again, what does it mean to you?

Grasp the marvelous significance of this Good News:

*You are living a brand new kind of life that is continually learning more and more of what is right, and trying constantly to be more and more like Christ who **created this new life within you**.* (Colossians 3:10)

We are trying constantly to be more and more like Christ!

I AM AN ADOPTED CHILD

And so we should not be like cringing, fearful slaves, but we should behave like God's very own children adopted into the bosom of his family, and calling to him, "Father, Father." (Romans 8:15)

We may have looked cute as babies when we were born, but we still had the potential to do bad things.

From Adam and Eve we inherited a desire to do what we want, when we want to do it.

We all have a tendency to do what we should not do. But we were also born with the potential to become the adopted children of God!

People can choose to adopt a child. That child then belongs to them. God chooses to adopt children and claims them as His own.

What if God desired to select only very good children? Some of us would not have a chance! But God does have very clear-cut criteria for the children He wants. He wants only those who choose to believe what Jesus tells us. Jesus tells us that God loves us so much that He wants to give us His Son's righteousness and everlasting life.

We will stand before God with Christ's righteousness. What could be better?

Do you believe you are an adopted child of God? God knows exactly what you believe!

An adopted child may not always feel like they are adopted. But what they feel does not change the reality of their status. When they are able to read they can see and read their adoption papers for themselves.

You can read with your own eyes the proof that God has adopted you. You can read His recording of your adoption! You can speak to Him and say, "My Father who art in Heaven!"

I am proud of my name "Carothers," but what if I was not proud? You might wonder what had happened to cause me to be ashamed of my ancestors. God has adopted me, but what if I told you I was not sure if I had been adopted? Would you think that I was ashamed to be called God's adopted son?

Are you God's adopted child?

HAVING FAITH

Before Jesus came, God gave a special mission to men and women who had faith in Him. Through these believers He kept emphasizing that we could not be pleasing to Him unless we learned to have faith in what He tells us.

Our understanding of faith becomes stronger as we study Jesus' life. He demonstrated the power of God so people would know they could trust Him no matter what happened. We too can learn from Him. That is difficult because we have learned, so well, not to believe anything we cannot see.

Most of us know we are far from perfect. What must happen before we can know that we imperfect ones are going to Heaven? Jesus said each person must become a new person – a born again person.

Without our doing anything we were born here on earth. In the same way we cannot make ourselves a new person. We must be changed by a power far greater than our own.

Here is what Paul wrote:

When someone becomes a Christian he becomes a brand new person inside. He is not the same any more. A new life has begun! (2 Corinthians 5:17)

God, the Creator of life, can create a new life in us. He didn't say, "If you become a better person I will make you a brand new person." Jesus explained God's plan this way:

I am the way and the truth and the life. No one comes to the Father except through me. (John 14:6 NIV)

We are unable to even come to God by our own efforts; we must come through our faith in His Son. Once we place our faith and trust in Jesus, He brings us to His Father.

WHAT GOD CAN DO

A rich religious ruler asked Jesus how he could go to Heaven. He told Jesus he had kept all the commandments since he was a young boy. Jesus did not contradict the man but told him that it was easier for a camel to go through the eye of a needle than for a rich man to enter Heaven. Then Jesus said to him:

Sell all you have and give the money to the poor – it will become treasure for you in heaven – and come, follow me. (Luke 18:22)

Those who heard Jesus asked:

How can anyone be saved? (Luke 18:26)

Jesus replied:

God can do what men can't! (Luke 18:27)

Yes, no matter what we do it is impossible for us to save ourselves, but God can easily make us His children!

THE PRODIGAL SON – PART I

Jesus told the parable of the Prodigal Son who wasted his inheritance on wine, women and song. Then the son heads back home to his father so he can repent, beg for forgiveness and offer to work as a slave. The father runs to meet him, embraces him, and plans a grand banquet in his son's honor. The son had expected his father to be angry, but his father rejoices to have his son home.

Regardless of what we have done, God will never be angry when we ask for His forgiveness.

The older brother in Jesus' parable becomes angry. He has been a faithful, hard working son, and now his father is honoring his brother.

You and I could be striving to please God but fail to realize that what He wants is our faith in His goodness! He wants to throw His arms around us and say, "I understand you. I love you. I see that you want to please me. I forgive you."

"But Father," we say, "I keep doing the wrong things. How can I claim to be Your son?"

Our Father responds, "I claim you. My Son paid the penalty for your sins. Believe what He tells you and you will be my child forever."

"But Father," we protest, "how can I tell anyone that I am yours? They know what a good child should be like."

"Just tell them about my love for anyone who believes in My Son as Savior," He assures us.

If we cling to our own righteousness, trying to be perfect, the Bible says we are living in bondage. When the spirit of the older brother rules in us we are basing our eternal salvation on ourselves rather than on God's love.

Any person who feels that he must be a better person in order to be God's child will forever strive to be that better person. Like the older son, He will never be able to receive the perfect love and forgiveness of our perfect Father. Our Father knows that we have inherited the sinful nature of Adam and Eve and He wants us to accept the gift of forgiveness that Jesus died to give us.

We suffer as a result of the sins of Adam and Eve as well as the sins of all our ancestors. Many people blame God for the painful things that happen to them. Many believe that in spite of their sinful nature they still have the potential to be good enough to make it to Heaven.

No person – ever – has been good enough to make it to Heaven. Yet Satan still convinces some that they should never claim to be sure they are going to Heaven. Our only hope is to believe what Jesus said.

THE PRODIGAL SON – PART II

We come to God in the same way that a bank robber or a murderer must come. God sees only our faith in His Son. If you have faith in Jesus as your Savior, tell God what you believe. Of course Satan and others will respond to you as the Prodigal Son's brother did. He thought it was unfair and ridiculous for his father to accept this wicked son who had spent his entire inheritance on wine, women and song while he had so faithfully served his father. But their father could do as he pleased – and he did.

People may tell you that you have no right to call yourself a child of God. They may say that you first need to pay for all your wasted years and become worthy of being called a Christian. Pay them no heed. Your Father has the final say about who you are and what He wants to do with you.

I have heard from prisoners serving a life sentence. My heart rejoices when they tell of the joy that flooded them when they realized God loved them. They were suddenly overwhelmed with joy when they repented and believed God's promises. Some of them had spent years wishing, over and over, that they had not committed crimes. The family and friends of some had declared them to be outcasts. Some had not heard from anyone for many years and spent many hours plotting suicide. But Jesus filled them with forgiveness and peace. Now they are telling their fellow prisoners about Jesus and others are experiencing the same forgiveness and joy. This is what happened when Jesus' disciples went from country to country telling people the Good News that Jesus had told them. Thousands of people who had been held in bondage were set free by Christ's message. They too went to city after city telling others what Jesus had said:

My purpose is to give life in all its fullness. (John 10:10)

Read it again: *My purpose is to give life in all its fullness.*

Jesus' gift does not come to those who feel they can earn righteousness if they just try a little harder. His gift comes to those who realize that they are totally dependent on Him.

We rest in the assurance that we are in Christ. We understand that we ourselves are not perfect:

For none of us is perfect! (Galatians 6:5)

We are not perfect but we can cling to this fact:

There is no condemnation awaiting those who belong to Christ Jesus. (Romans 8:1)

Please do not try to become so pleasing to God that He will overlook your failure to believe that Jesus is your Savior both now and forever. If even one person could meet God's requirement by their deeds, then they would prove that it is possible for anyone to do the same.

In order for Jesus to be our Savior He had to live a perfect, sinless life to satisfy God's declaration that no imperfect person could enter Heaven. Otherwise Heaven would be polluted. Jesus gives His righteousness to those who receive His gift!

For God was in Christ, restoring the world to Himself, no longer counting men's sins against them but blotting them out. This is the wonderful message he has given us to tell others. (2 Corinthians 5:19)

You may have noticed that I frequently repeat this same truth. My lifetime of helping people who are bogged down by their fear of not being good enough, prompts me to list Scriptures that emphasize our salvation by faith in Jesus. You may have heard them but for some reason have never received them for yourself. Right now is your best opportunity.

If you believe in the Good News, remember that there are many around you who do not know what it is! Many!

Many people don't have an understanding of what the Good News is. They may have heard it but for some reason have never received it for themselves.

PRODIGAL SON – PART III

The Prodigal son's father ordered a huge celebration. His son was home! The very best food was to be prepared.

When we receive God's full and complete forgiveness, there is a joyous celebration!

Unbelievers cannot comprehend that righteousness is given to us as a free gift. But we know this to be the Good News that Jesus came to give us.

Jesus was crucified because He claimed to be The Son of God, the Messiah. You and I make no such claim, but we do profess that God has given us eternal life. We also assert that He has given us His righteousness and made us His children.

Such claims can stir men's wrath. That's why Jesus was persecuted and crucified. That's why many early Christians were executed.

We must see Jesus as qualified to be in Heaven, the One who is absolutely perfect and without sin and as the One who gave His life in order to give us God's forgiveness. Without Him we know that we have no hope or assurance of ever being able to stand in God's presence. We know that no matter how hard we try we can never be good enough. We are rejoicing in what Jesus has done for us. Yes, I know I have said this before but we need to repeat this to ourselves over and over because Satan will tell us over and over that we are not good enough.

THE PRODIGAL SON – PART IV

The natural instinct of a person who has failed to live a perfect life is to think of ways to redeem themselves: "I will do better. I will stay out of trouble."

The Prodigal Son did not have an opportunity to make any excuses. When he was still a long way off his father saw him and reacted as a father who loves His son.

The elder son represents those who have never gotten into serious trouble and look down on those who have. They do not understand:

We are all infected and impure with sin. When we put on our prized robes of righteousness we find they are but filthy rags. (Isaiah 64:6)

They also do not understand what Paul says about faith:

I have put aside all else, counting it worthless than nothing, in order that I can have Christ, and become one with him, no longer counting on being saved by being good enough or by obeying God's laws, but by trusting Christ to save me; for God's way of making us right with himself depends on faith – counting on Christ alone. (Philippians 3:8-9)

THE PRODIGAL SON – PART V

Jesus told stories to help us understand God, stories such as "The Prodigal Son." The story is really about God and how He treats a sinner who repents.

The Prodigal Son represents many of us. He asked for his inheritance and went to another land where he squandered everything his father had given him. When he realized his mistake, he hoped his father might accept him back as a servant and he went back home. His father planned a banquet to celebrate his son's return. The older brother represents those who do not believe in salvation by faith. He chastised his younger brother and his father. Why? He had been faithful to his father and had worked hard all his life. He thought that he should be honored, not his lazy brother.

The father, who represents God, couldn't help but rejoice when his son returned. He said:

This son of mine was dead and has returned to life. He was lost and is found. (Luke 15:24)

Jesus wants us to understand God's love for us so we will love Him. He always welcomes us when we come to Him. Our enemy wants us to think that God requires us to be perfect. You may relate to the younger son and think that you must be a better person in order to be accepted by God. But God accepts us whenever we come to Him. We must believe that:

God loved the world so much that he gave his only Son so that anyone who believes in him shall not perish but have eternal life. (John 3:16)

If we are asked, "Are you going to Heaven?" we should answer "YES!" Be aware that when we do this, those who are like the elder son will declare that we do not deserve to say such a proud and grandiose thing about ourselves.

DYING BESIDE JESUS

One of the murderers dying beside Jesus believed that Jesus could take him to Heaven. He said:

Jesus, remember me when you come into your Kingdom. (Luke 23:42)

Jesus' response was:

Today you will be with me in paradise. (Luke 23:43)

Was the thief taken to Heaven? If you say "yes," why was he granted such easy entrance when he admitted that he deserved to be crucified? If a soldier had taken him off the cross before he died, would he still go to Heaven? If so, why? He would go to heaven because he believed Jesus could do this for him. Jesus said He would.

Jesus promised that you and I would be with Him in Heaven forever if we believe what He promised us. Do you believe Him? If so, you should say, "I know I will go to Heaven. I am going there because of what He said and did, not because of anything I have done. I could never open the gates into Heaven. Only the Son of God could do that."

The thief believed and the doors were opened!

DO I DESERVE HEAVEN?

What if God asked me, "Merlin, have you obeyed Me perfectly since I forgave you and had your name written in Heaven?"

"No," I would have to answer.

"Merlin, do you deserve to enter Heaven?"

"No, I do not."

"Merlin, do you believe I will permit you to enter?"

"Yes, I am sure that You will!"

"Why do you say that?"

"Because You promised that if I believed in Jesus as my Savior, I would go to Heaven."

"Merlin, why do you think I gave you that promise?"

"Because You love me."

I know that in spite of all my shortcomings and failures this is what Jesus promises us. He said:

Though all heaven and earth shall pass away, yet my words remain forever true. (Luke 21:33)

Are you unsure about what you believe? My own assurance is based on what Jesus teaches us. I have found no better source.

Trying to be good enough to make it to Heaven is like trying to fly by flapping our arms in the breeze. It just doesn't work.

If we think we might be the one human who can learn how to be good enough, we face overwhelming odds. In fact, impossible odds. Trusting in God to give us the righteousness of Jesus as a free gift is the solution.

Long before Jesus came to the earth, God saw that He was the only way for men and women to be fit for Heaven. Thank You, Father, for loving us that much.

MOVING A MOUNTAIN

Jesus said we could move a mountain even if we had faith as small as a mustard seed. What did He mean? Should we seek the faith to move a mountain?

A mustard seed will grow if it is properly cared for. Faith of any size will grow if we give it the opportunity to do so.

We should try to increase our faith for the right reasons, to accomplish what God wants us to accomplish.

For example, believe that you will not be irritable for the next five minutes. Have faith that you will not be worried, anxious, frustrated or upset by anything that comes your way today. When you are successful believe that you can do it again. Keep believing and see the new confidence that builds in you!

If you know you need to go for a walk to improve your health but you do not feel like doing it, get yourself ready and then walk a short distance. Rejoice in what you can do, and if possible, walk a little more. Believe that you will be able to do a little more tomorrow. Let your confidence grow! This will bless both you and God.

I regularly walk up two hills while quoting to myself, *Be strong in the Lord, and in the power of His might* (Ephesians 6:10 KJV). My shoulders pull back and I sense His might moving in me.

Believe that your health is one percent better, or even one quarter of one percent better. Keep doing this regardless of how you feel. Your objective is to believe that you can do it. With God's help you can. There are so many things that we can do to demonstrate our desire to grow in faith.

BAD HABITS

What is a bad habit? Is it something that we want to be delivered from or something that God has declared bad? Our sinful minds may decide that we, not God, should have the right to decide what is good or bad.

Often people decide that they want to be delivered from a bad habit, so they ask God to deliver them. They pray over and over. Then they decide that if God wanted them to be delivered He would have answered their prayer, and with this excuse they go back to enjoying their bad habit.

Why doesn't God deliver us from harmful habits? Does He prefer to let us suffer? I have watched and heard many people wrestle with a difficult problem while that very same problem destroys them. Yes, God could deliver us from anything. But He gave us free will. He also gave us His written Word and clear evidence that what He says is right and good.

Alcohol, when consumed, creates a craving. Anyone can find proof that this craving destroys millions of lives. But Satan blinds people so that they see, but they don't see. Those who remain blind may blame God. He often refuses to deliver men from something that they choose to enjoy.

There are many "forbidden fruits" that men refuse to give up. They suffer and cause family and friends to suffer. Drugs, pornography, and homosexual addictions often hide behind their conviction that God is responsible for their problems. They declare that they are the way they are because God created them that way. God permits their behavior but He does not accept it. His Word says that our way will be hard and He will not bless us if we disobey. But if we strive with God's help to break a bad habit, He will deliver us. He longs to set us free from everything that Satan has led us into.

God has healed people from addictions as I prayed for them. Why? Not because of anything in me! This was what He wanted to do. He would have done the same for any Christian who prayed and believed Him.

DEFEATING BAD HABITS

Satan convinces some folks that their bad habit is too difficult to break. But it is not too difficult if we know what to do.

Using our own will power to break a habit is usually difficult. Every cell in our body can work against us. The body says, "I want to do what I want to do so I can enjoy myself!" The mind cooperates and says, "I would stop if I could but I can't."

So what alternatives do we have? Try Jesus' way. He said to ask and believe. In yourself? No! In God. What do you have to lose?

Nearly every doctor agrees that stress is harmful. It causes our heart to be nervous and that could lead to a heart attack. Easier to see is the damage that bad habits can do to our lives.

The Bible is a wonderful book of healing. It tells us to trust, be glad, to rejoice always, not to fret and not to worry. If you do not want the bother of striving to break a bad habit, think about the benefits of living by what God tells you. If you think you cannot do that, find ways to grow in faith.

These daily devotions could give you faith to believe that God is delivering you from yourself and from the horrible pains that bad habits bring.

NEVER GIVE UP

Doctors often ask, "On a scale of 1 to 10 how bad do you feel?" We decide how we feel. What is our decision based on? We often decide how to answer based on how we have answered in the past. Once our mind is programmed, it makes the same decision over and over.

We can become programmed to believe that God wants us to do something even if that is not what He wants us to do! For example, we may pray ten times a day for God to help us do something. The next day we may repeat the same prayer eleven times. But our real goal is not to keep asking, it is to learn how to believe that God is helping us. Believing brings confidence and joy. Unbelieving prayers do not bring joy. If your prayers leave you unhappy, learn to pray in a way that will cause you to grow in the joy of the Lord. Paul tells us in Ephesians 6:18 to:

Pray in the Spirit.

Ask Him to give you the words that you should pray.

"God, what should I do to be sure I will go to Heaven?" We can repeat such a prayer over and over until asking increases our doubts.

When people tried to get near Jesus so He would heal them, He saw their faith and healed them. We too can get closer to Jesus and He will see our faith!

God responds to our faith. Therefore, our objective is to grow in faith. This book offers many suggestions of what you can do. Don't give up. God would not tell us to believe Him if we did not have the ability to do so. He sent His Holy Spirit to live in us and to help us believe. We have to learn in the same way that a little baby does. A baby tries and tries and keeps on trying until the moment comes when it can walk. In time the child will learn to run. Then the child will learn to ride a bicycle, swim, fly an airplane, graduate from college, and on and on.

Each step forward requires our own determination and God's help. God does what we cannot do.

Never give up. Each step forward brings us closer to the objective God has for us. He wants us to keep growing in faith!

WORLD WAR II

In World War II, I served with the 82nd Airborne Division in Belgium, France and Germany. What did we do when it seemed we were being defeated? We tried harder. If one tactic didn't work we tried something else. Every unit, large or small, was responsible to do whatever was necessary to win.

At the same time our enemy was determined to defeat us.

Satan is determined to defeat us. If one tactic doesn't work he will try another. To win he knows he must destroy our trust in God.

During combat it sometimes became completely silent. That was not a time for us to relax. Our enemy could be quiet so we would relax. Then they could creep quietly and unseen toward us. That is why Satan does not want us to be aware that he even exists. Jesus knew he was real and urged us to be aware of his tactics

We win our spiritual battles when we keep fighting. Even when we are fighting a battle we can experience peace. We don't need to worry because we can trust God. Jesus told us:

I am leaving you with a gift – peace of mind and heart! And the peace I give isn't fragile like the peace the world gives. So don't be troubled or afraid. (John 14:27)

His gifts may seem difficult to receive but when we have faith in what He promised, He will give us peace of heart and mind!

MY STRENGTH

The Lord is my fort where I can enter and be safe; no one can follow me in and slay me. He is a rugged mountain where I hide; he is my Savior, a rock where none can reach me, and a tower of safety. He is my shield. He is like the strong horn of a mighty fighting bull. (Psalms 18:2)

Most people who want eternal life are

tempted to think that if they try hard enough to be a better person they can make it. But that cannot be done. We must put all our trust in God. He is the one who gives salvation to anyone who believes that He loves us that much.

Think of how you will feel when you believe that God gives you His strength! You will no longer be handicapped by your own weakness. That's what Jesus taught His disciples to feel and believe:

I can do everything God asks me to with the help of Christ who gives me the strength and power. (Philippians 4:13)

Try to realize what you can do through Christ who gives you His strength. By His power working in you, you can help others to trust in His strength. This is what He asked His disciples to do. They believed Him and were used to influence the entire world!

Believing does not depend on our circumstances! While he was chained in prison, Paul wrote encouraging letters to Christians when they were discouraged. God is still using these prison letters to change the hearts of men all over the world.

PEACE

When we *strive to live a good life* we know that we will eventually fail to be as good as we would like to be.

God observed many generations of His creation and He saw how impossible it was for people to always do the right thing. But God was willing to come to earth, as Jesus, and to live a perfect, holy life. Jesus endured the same temptations that we face but He lived the perfect life that God requires of anyone who is to enter Heaven:

This High Priest of ours understands our weaknesses, for he faced all of the same temptations we do, yet he did not sin. (Hebrews 4:15) That fact is not difficult for us to believe. But many people find it very difficult to believe that Jesus actually offers to give His righteousness as a free gift, just because He loves us.

If we are anxious, worried or troubled by our failures, our peace of heart is being determined by our own deeds and not by what Jesus does for us. Until we accept Christ's peace as our own, Satan will cause us to reject what Jesus offers. Our faith in what He has done can cause His peace to rule and reign in us. And with that comes new love for God and an ever-increasing desire to be pleasing to Him.

LIFE AS IT REALLY IS

If you are wondering whether I know anything about life as it really is, remember this: I served in World War II, Korea, Vietnam and the Dominican Republic. I was knocked unconscious many times. I've had failures and frustrations. The one thing I am sure of is that Jesus has always been there to deliver me. Each time God delivered me my confidence grew stronger that He will never fail me or forsake me.

For God has said, "I will never, never fail you nor forsake you." (Hebrews 13:5)

WHEN SATAN TEMPTS US

I have learned that when Satan tempts me I have the most powerful defense that anyone could have. I am free to say to him, "I am God's child. He loves me regardless of any accusations you make against me. In Jesus' name, leave me alone."

At first I was timid because Satan is powerful. But as I grow stronger in faith and in the knowledge of how much God loves His children, I become bolder in what I say. This causes my faith to grow even more.

I recommend that you do not challenge Satan until you believe that you are God's adopted child. When we are bold against Satan, in Jesus' name, we become a little more like Jesus!

God is the same for everyone who believes Him. Do you see how important it is to learn everything you can about the miracle working power of faith in Jesus? Doubting His Son does not please God! He wants us to live in this way:

Shrinking back from all that might displease Him. (Philippians 2:12)

Most of us have known Christians who made bad mistakes. Why did they do these things? Satan tempted them!

Be careful – watch out for attacks from Satan, your great enemy. He prowls around like a hungry, roaring lion, looking for some victim to tear apart. (1 Peter 5:8)

Peter suffered great agony after he denied even knowing Jesus. He had been tempted and he felt as if he had been torn apart. Satan will tempt anyone who is trying to please God.

The only way I can enter Heaven is to be perfect. I'm not perfect. If I live hundreds of years I will not be able to become perfect. But I have received the perfect righteousness of Jesus as a free gift. For now, I will just try my best to learn how to become a little more like Him.

There are many things that we will never achieve unless we believe we can.

Why does anyone believe that they can do something? They believe because something or someone helped them to believe. We can believe that we are God's children, and we can believe that we will be victorious when Satan tempts us. Jesus came to help us believe!

OUR MOST POWERFUL RESOURCE

Faith in God is our most powerful resource. We may fail. Others may fail us. But God never fails.

Because we don't see Him we may not realize what He does for us. Men and women in the Bible say they saw God do things, so we may wonder why we do not.

Jesus and His disciples answered that question. They told us to keep our eyes and attention off everything in this world. That seems like an impossible goal, but Jesus' disciples eventually did reach that goal. They gave up a natural desire for the things they wanted and replaced all those desires with faith in God. As a result God gave them everything. They received a certainty that God was preparing them for eternity.

Jesus could have asked God to spare Him from suffering but instead He chose to trust that God would do whatever was best. His disciples could have prayed to be released from prison, from being beaten and stoned, but they chose to have faith that God was working good for them. As a result they have done more for the world than any men and women who have ever lived.

Satan hates revealing himself to anyone but he became so frustrated that he appeared to Jesus. He could not frighten or deceive Jesus. We can have faith in Jesus because He lived a human life without sin, and we have His Spirit within us!

You and I can believe that God will permit nothing to happen that He will not use for our good. Yes, this takes faith. But faith is our most powerful resource! So why not build our faith by believing that Jesus has given us the free gift of eternal life?

THE VOICE OF TRIUMPH

The Holy Spirit quoted Psalm 47:1 to me in a forceful way when I was lounging on an easy chair:

Clap your hands, all ye people; shout unto God with the voice of triumph.

The Holy Spirit often uses Scripture to get our attention.

At 87 I sometimes feel very tired when I wake up. Of course I have all kinds of reasons.

On this particular day I wanted to sit in

my lounge chair, in my pajamas, and snooze before doing anything. But fortunately I am learning obedience. I began to shout to God, in my mind, words of praise and victory.

I still felt tired. But then I realized that I was not being "triumphant," so I acted triumphantly by simply putting my clothes on.

Then I walked up a nearby hill that is always a challenge to me. To my joy and delight each step brought new joy. I sensed the Holy Spirit saying, "See!"

Since then I keep this verse in the front of my mind regardless of what my ancient brain tells me. God is causing His Word to work in me in a new way. Whether I'm working or just walking, I often remember those words, "Shout unto God with the voice of triumph." This helps me to practice believing that God's Word is designed to help us.

I know that an unbelieving world would say I am only enjoying mind over matter. I also know that God gave us our minds and intends for us to use them for good. In the Bible the word "mind" or "minds" is used 118 times. A few of these are:

1. *And Moses said, "Hereby ye shall know that the Lord hath sent me to do all these works; for I have not done them of mine own mind."* (Numbers 16:28 KJV)

God speaks to us through our minds.

2. *Solomon, my son, get to know the God*

of your fathers. Worship and serve him with a clean heart and a willing mind, for the Lord sees every heart and understands and knows every thought. If you seek him, you will find him. (1 Chronicles 28:9)

3. *Don't copy the behavior and customs of this world, but let God transform you into a new person by changing the way you think. Then you will know what God wants you to do and you will know how good and pleasing and perfect his will really is.* (Romans 12:2)

4. *Be made new in the attitude of your minds.* (Ephesians 4:23 NIV)

5. *And the peace of God, which passeth all understanding, shall keep your hearts and minds through Christ Jesus.* (Philippians 4:7 KJV)

JOB

My offenses will be sealed up in a bag; you will cover over my sin. (Job 14:17 NIV)

This is a graphic picture of what God does for those who believe His promises.

The book of Job is believed to be the first book of the Bible ever written. Here we learn about God's nature and what He wants to see in us:

There lived in the land of Uz a man named Job – a good man who feared God and stayed away from evil. (Job 1:1)

Satan asked for God's permission to torment this blameless and upright man. God gave Satan permission to attack Job.

Job lost all of his possessions. His friends accused him of some secret sin. His own wife thought he was to blame.

All of his children died.

Then God permitted Satan to cover Job's body with boils! Even one boil is terrible. Job's response to all of this suffering was:

Though He slay me, yet will I trust in Him. (Job 13:15 KJV)

God said to Satan:

He has kept his faith in me despite the fact that you persuaded Me to let you harm him without any cause. (Job 2:3)

Job's suffering was severe but he became a living example for you and me. Satan can get permission to cause us suffering but when we refuse to doubt God we too will be God's witness for now and for eternity.

God wants us to·trust Him regardless of what Satan does. When we trust God, He will eventually reveal His plan and purpose for everything that happened between Adam and Eve and the final end of planet earth.

While we are here Satan may ask, "Are you sure you are going to Heaven?" We need to know why we are sure. That's what this book is all about!

STRUGGLING TO HAVE FAITH

Zechariah and Elizabeth were upright in the sight of God. The Scriptures go so far as to say that they were blameless. The angel Gabriel appeared to Zechariah and told him that Elizabeth would have a son. Zechariah did not believe the angel because both he and Elizabeth were both very old.

Gabriel told Zechariah that he would be unable to speak until the baby was born. Even a "blameless" man found it difficult to believe God. Because of his unbelief he temporarily lost the ability to speak. How much greater will the consequences be if we refuse to believe that Jesus is our Savior – for both this life and the life to come?

At times even Jesus' disciples struggled to have faith.

Jesus' disciples were very much like us. They had families, homes and businesses. But after they had listened to Jesus and had seen His miracles, they left everything and followed Him. Did they have complete faith in Him? No, they simply had enough faith to follow Him. Eventually they too were able to perform great miracles. But when small or severe problems came they had more to learn about trusting Him.

We too have much to learn and that is why we need to go over and over the Scriptures.

Jesus knew that His disciples would desert Him when He was arrested, tortured and crucified. But He still loved them. He was willing and prepared to give Himself as a sacrifice for every sin that they, and we, would commit. God knows our human nature! We need the nature of His perfect Son, which can be ours through faith. We will never be able to destroy God's plan. How glad that makes me. I know myself well enough to know that I have made mistakes, will continue to make mistakes, and would even make mistakes in Heaven if God didn't have a different plan! In Heaven I will not be the Merlin I know. But even here on earth God has made provision for me through Christ. Paul wrote:

Christ Jesus . . . is at the right hand of God and is also interceding for us. (Romans 8:34 NIV)

Are you struggling to have faith? When you think of how bad you are, or have been, be sure to think of Jesus standing before God. He will intercede for everyone who believes He is their Savior!

Paul asks:

Who shall separate us from the love of Christ? Shall trouble or hardship or perse-cution or famine or nakedness or danger or sword? No, in all these things we are more than conquerors through him who loved us. (Romans 8:35, 37 NIV)

Once we have made our decision to trust in Jesus we do not need to fear that He will ever disown us!

SERVING GOD

John the Baptist proved to be the man called by God to announce the coming of Jesus. He fulfilled his mission, but as a result Herod placed him in prison. Then Herod's wife convinced her daughter to do a sensual dance before Herod and his friends. The dance so stirred Herod's desires that he offered to give the girl anything she wanted. She asked for, and was given, the head of John the Baptist.

Why would God permit John to be beheaded? Serving God may lead to suffering. But the writer of Hebrews encourages us to follow Jesus' example:

Keep your eyes on Jesus, our leader and instructor. He was willing to die a shameful death on the cross because of the joy he knew would be his afterwards; and now he sits in the place of honor by the throne of God. (Hebrews 12:2)

You may be tempted to question God's love if you are having problems or see others suffering. Do not succumb to Satan's temptations. God used Jesus' death to bring eternal life to you. His resurrection proved that His words were true. Because we believed His words we will one day hear God say, *Well done thou good and faithful servant.* (Matthew 25:21)

USED BY GOD

I was walking beside the church that Mary and I attend, talking with one of the very active members. I was telling her what a wonderful job she is doing to help many people. She was laughing and saying she wished she could do more. A young lady was coming toward us and the lady beside me stopped her and said, "This is Merlin Carothers, do you know him?" Then the young lady surprised me by saying. "Do I know him? I sure do. God used him to change my life! I used to be so unhappy and now I'm happy all the time. I sing and dance (she began to dance in front of us) and when I see a problem coming I start praising God for it. Thank you, thank you Merlin."

How do you think that made me feel? I wanted to dance with the young lady! Her joy gave me joy. I wanted to get back home and write this section so you would know that God is still working. He is causing us to rejoice, to share our joy with others, and causing others to want the joy that He gives us.

As we parted I was laughing in my mind about what God has done in me.

Many, oh so many times I have been walking in the wrong direction. Had I continued following that path Satan would have destroyed me. But since God wrote my name in His book of eternal life He has loved and protected me as His son. Over and over He has kept His promise to never leave me or forsake me. God loves me and has never treated me, as I deserved to be treated, but rather as His son.

Yes, God has permitted me to suffer because He loves me and wants me to learn how much I need His love.

Are you tempted to feel defeated? Yes, you may be tempted, but if your faith is in Jesus you are God's beloved child!

There are people who need your help. Let them see God working in you so they will laugh, skip and rejoice over what they know God has done for them.

Don't ever think, "But I am not good enough for God to use me." God wants to use everyone. Have the incredible joy of believing that He will use you. How will He use you? Let Him decide! Then you can do the enjoying.

ABRAHAM

God honored Abraham as a man of faith. But his faith had to be tested:

While God was testing him, Abraham still trusted in God and his promises, and so he offered up his son Isaac, and was ready to slay him on the altar of sacrifice. (Hebrews 11:17)

If we say, "I believe in Jesus," God wants us to demonstrate our faith:

Just as the body is dead when there is no spirit in it, so faith is dead if it is not the kind that results in good deeds. (James 2:26)

Remember – God honors what we believe, but what we do demonstrates what we believe.

We are called to tell the world about Jesus. Faith in Him is important! If you want more of God's help don't make the mistake of only asking for His help: do what He told us to do. Tell others what He has done for you.

JOHN 3:16

When we were born we had no control over the appearance or health of our body. We had to accept whatever our ancestors passed on to us. But we do have control over the person we become.

We can choose the easiest path or we can

choose whatever will improve our future. Improving our future would be an intelligent decision. We can also learn what our Creator wants us to do.

Jesus knew exactly what God wants us to do. He told us that nothing is as important as learning to love God. In order to love God we must understand His love for us. Jesus said in John 3:16:

For God loved the world so much that he gave his only Son so that anyone who believes in him shall not perish but have eternal life.

Think of that enormous promise – everlasting life! Whoever believes has everlasting life! That promise is what Satan does not want anyone to believe.

Many people are familiar with John 3:16, but few know the verse that follows it:

God did not send his Son into the world to condemn it, but to save it. (John 3:17)

God's purpose in sending His Son was to save the world! He loves us that much.

How thankful should we be for God's Son?

We will not be **very thankful** if we are not sure what He did for us. If we are unsure, we might spend our entire lives just wondering what He did for us and why. That does not lead to loving God.

Satan doesn't want us to understand what Jesus has done for us. He will do anything to prevent us from believing that God loves us and that faith in Jesus gives us absolute assurance that we will be with Him for eternity.

You love him even though you have never seen him; though not seeing him, you trust him; and even now you are happy with the inexpressible joy that comes from heaven itself. And your further reward for trusting him will be the salvation of your souls. (1 Peter 1:8-9)

Loving God is what we were created for. Do you see how crucial it is that we believe John 3:16?

BACK TO LIFE

God brought Jesus back to life and we share in that life:

When God the Father, with glorious power, brought him back to life again, you were given his wonderful new life to enjoy. (Romans 6:4)

We are now:

Free under God's favor and mercy. (Romans 6:14)

We have God's free gift of:

Eternal life through Christ Jesus our Lord. (Romans 6:23)

We have new life in Christ! This is cause for rejoicing! Why is it hard for us to rejoice? Why don't we live like we are free and under God's mercy?

We still wrestle with the problem that Paul had. We want to always do what is right but at times we fail. Satan will tell us that we could not possibly be God's children if we do such imperfect things. Paul declared that there was nothing good in him. He wanted us to know that our goodness exists totally in Christ. There is nothing good in us. We were born that way.

When we were young and needed to do something, our flesh said, "I don't feel like doing it." We were too busy or we just knew we didn't want to do it.

Now if our flesh hears, "Rejoice in the Lord always," or "Shout unto God with the voice of triumph," the flesh says, "Ridiculous." But the spirit of Jesus who lives in us still says, "Rejoice. Shout for joy. Use the power that I have given you."

A movie actor can shout with a voice of triumph, for no reason other than to win an award and to earn money. How much more should we who have eternal life rejoice in the Lord?

We cannot, of course, shout that we are triumphant if we do not mean what we are saying. How then do we believe we are triumphant when many things seem to be going wrong? We must learn to believe what God tells us!

PETER, BEFORE AND AFTER

After Jesus was arrested, another of His disciples brought Peter into the courtyard where Jesus was being held. A girl on duty there asked Peter if he was one of Jesus' disciples. Peter answered:

I am not! (John. 18:17)

Twice more that night Peter denied that he was a disciple. One denial often leads to another. But there is hope for all of us. Soon after this episode Peter became a mighty witness for Christ and caused thousands of people to believe in Jesus as their Savior.

With all the earnestness that I possess, I promise you that when you give Jesus the praise and thanksgiving that He deserves, God will be pleased with you. In all your life there will be nothing you can do to please God more than to honor His Son by your faith in what He has done for you.

When I was invited to be the guest speaker at Carnegie Hall in New York City it was because the sponsor saw that I really believed what I had written in my books. Why have my books been translated and published in 59 languages? Because readers saw that I really believed and I helped them to believe.

You are called by God to help people believe in Jesus! You and I need to do whatever we can to strengthen our faith.

Satan's primary objective is to prevent Jesus from being exalted by anyone. You can do nothing more pleasing to God than to clearly proclaim to others that Jesus is your Savior and wants to be their Savior too.

WHAT IS YOUR FOUNDATION?

The events of our lives have influenced what we believe is right and what is wrong. On what do you base your beliefs?

You may believe one thing and I may believe the opposite. Which belief is correct? We need a solid foundation to determine what is correct.

The Bible is my foundation. I don't always understand it perfectly but my goal is to live my life by what the Bible says. To do that, I need to know what it says! This book is my effort to help you know what the Bible says about God's plan.

The events of our lives have also helped us decide what we think we must do in order to go to Heaven. Please carefully consider what the Bible declares to be true. It has been read, studied and preached for thousands of years. Many men have tried to prove that it is not true, but their reasons have been disproved by thousands of scholars, teachers, readers and believers. Other religions offer rules, regulations, self-efforts and sacrifices that leave believers with none of the joy, peace and happiness that Jesus came to give us.

What is your foundation?

I MUST LEAVE YOU

When Jesus told His disciples that He was going to leave them, they had the same reaction that many of us have when we learn something that displeases us. We ask "Why?"

Jesus' response to His disciples is the same as His response to you and me:

You are only filled with sorrow. But the fact of the matter is that it is best for you that I go away, for if I don't, the Comforter won't come. If I do, he will – for I will send him to you. (John 16:6-7)

Remember that the disciples didn't understand Jesus when He told them the Holy Spirit would come to help them. The Holy Spirit is here! We must learn to hear Him.

Jesus repeatedly emphasized that by believing God's Good News we will be given new lives and experience peace. We are continually tempted to disregard the peace that Jesus promised us. We may think that the temptations and problems of this world are so strong that we cannot live in His peace. Jesus said:

I have told you all this so that you will have peace of heart and mind. Here on earth you will have many trials and sorrows; but cheer up, for I have overcome the world. (John 16:33)

Jesus overcame for us what we could never overcome! The Holy Spirit is here to help us believe what Jesus promised. We can learn to hear the Holy Spirit. Listen to Him and He will help you to be delivered from things that trouble you. That will give you ever-increasing "peace of heart."

MOVING MOUNTAINS

During my four years in Christian colleges and three years in Seminary my professors told me – and convinced me – that there were talents I did not have. They were right. They said they believed that I tried my best to write good research papers and to speak before the class. They also said I couldn't express myself well on paper and had a speech problem but they believed I had other talents. But all the professors said I excelled in one thing: zeal. Of course in an academic setting students do not want zeal, they want high grades. I made it through with average grades. I confess that at first this made me feel inferior.

Later I found Bible verses that encouraged me. God doesn't grade us according to the values that we consider most important! He has His own grading system. For example:

Anything is possible if you have faith. (Mark 9:23)

And:

If you had faith even as small as a tiny mustard seed you could say to this mountain, "Move!" and it would go far away. Nothing would be impossible. (Matthew 17:20)

The one thing I needed to do was:

Make the most of every opportunity you have for doing good. (Ephesians 5:16)

God helped me to believe I could do that! When I've done my best to make the most of every opportunity, He has helped me to do what He planned for me.

Nobody but we ourselves can prevent us from doing the best we can. God will move the mountains!

NOW HEAR THIS

Hear this exhortation in Jude 1:20:

But you, dear friends, must build up your lives ever more strongly upon the foundation of our holy faith, learning to pray in the power and strength of the Holy Spirit.

There is great benefit in learning how to pray *in the power and strength of the Holy Spirit.* He helps us learn when and how to pray. As Jesus said:

When the Father sends the Comforter instead of me – and by the Comforter I mean the Holy Spirit – he will teach you much, as well as remind you of everything I myself have told you. (John 14:26)

He is the One who teaches us.

There is so much for us to learn. We learn by our faith in what Jesus taught us.

We also need to understand the methods of Jesus' enemy. Satan's tactic is to say, "Since you live by faith, and not by works, then you should be able to do anything you want and trust God to forgive you." Sounds good to some, but the Holy Spirit teaches a different message.

The Holy Spirit always leads us to live holy, pure lives. If we try to do this but fail He is always available to help us have a stronger desire to be pure.

SATAN'S TACTICS

What character in the Bible do you believe is most frequently mentioned? I haven't counted the references to all of them, but *Satan* and *Devil* are mentioned:

Satan: 53 times

Devil: 59 times

How frequently do you hear the name of Satan mentioned in non-Christian circles?

Probably very few. Why? He does not want anyone to think about his presence!

You have probably overheard someone being damned in God's name, but how many times in Satan's name? Perhaps never! He wants to keep his name out of our thoughts. Secrecy is highly important in any war.

Satan may convince you and me to do something that we should not do. But Jesus, who would not be influenced by evil of any kind, always defeated him:

When the devil had ended all the temptations, he left Jesus for a while and went away. (Luke 4:13)

Think of the significance of that occasion. Jesus defeated the best temptations that Satan could come up with. But Satan did not give up: he still believed that there was some way he would win.

Don't think that you can tell Satan never to tempt you. He will always persist and maneuver for a better opportunity. His most persistent temptation is to convince you that you are not good enough to be sure you are going to Heaven. Otherwise you will want to tell others that they can be sure too! (And you may want to tell others to read this book).

Jesus' disciples did succumb to what Satan whispered to them. Satan even caused Peter to tell Jesus what He should do! But Jesus turned and said to Peter:

Get thee behind me, Satan. (Matthew 16:23 KJV)

As Peter grew in the power of the Holy Spirit, he became increasingly aware of what Satan was trying to do. **You and I can do that too!**

NO CONDEMNATION

If God wanted to find some way to condemn us, it would be an easy task. He would have no difficulty in showing us many things that we are doing wrong.

For example, God told us not to judge other people. But we are often guilty of doing just that. Perhaps we don't mean to, but nevertheless we are breaking His rules. We are told to love others as much as we love ourselves. We may try to do this but more often than not we love ourselves more. Is there any hope for us?

Yes, the Good News of the Gospel – this is our hope! This is our reason to rejoice:

There is now no condemnation awaiting those who belong to Christ Jesus. (Romans 8:1)

We are declared "not guilty." How could this possibly be? There are many things for which we could expect God to condemn us. The Good News is that Christ died for our sins and gave us His righteousness! This is the miracle that stirs our hearts to sing and make melody. This miracle motivates us to tell God's Good News to people all over the world.

For thousands of years God had seen that men could or would not obey Him. No matter how abundantly He blessed people they repeatedly turned away from Him and refused to be obedient. But God had a plan. He sent His Son Jesus and said we would go to Heaven if we believe in Him as our Savior. He asks us to believe in His goodness, not our own. Once we do that His Holy Spirit works miracles in us. We discover a growing passion to be obedient:

We aren't saved from sin's grasp by knowing the commandments of God, because we can't and don't keep them, but God put into effect a different plan to save us. He sent his own Son in a human body like ours – except that ours are sinful – and destroyed sin's control over us by giving himself as a sacrifice for our sins. So now we can obey God's laws if we follow after the Holy Spirit and no longer obey the old evil nature within us. (Romans 8:3-4)

We have a new relationship with the Creator of the entire universe! We no longer stand condemned before him.

And so we should not be like cringing, fearful slaves, but we should behave like God's very own children, adopted into the bosom of his family, and calling to him, "Father, Father." (Romans 8:15)

Now the Holy Spirit can lead us, just as Jesus promised. We can learn to hear the voice of the Holy Spirit:

For his Holy Spirit speaks to us deep in our hearts, and tells us that we really are God's children. (Romans 8:16). (Learn to hear Him).

How could we possibly find adequate reason to disbelieve what God has done for us?

We discern that a person loves us by their attitude and actions toward us. What more could they do if they loved us with all their heart, demonstrating their love over and over, but we still refused to believe them?

NOT GOOD ENOUGH

What should we do if we are absolutely certain that we are not good enough to go to Heaven? Would it be truthful to say we are Christians?

All of us must decide if we will trust in our own goodness or rely completely on Christ's righteousness. Before we decide, we do need to consider if we believe that:

Salvation is not a reward for the good we have done, so none of us can take any credit for it. (Ephesians 2:9)

Knowing that we are not good enough to be called Christians is a blessing because only the self-righteous would claim to be good enough to enter a perfect, holy Heaven. Humans of any variety would corrupt Heaven if God did not do something to cleanse and purify them before they entered their eternal home.

So rejoice if you feel unworthy! Rejoice when you have received God's gift of His Son's righteousness. Right now is a good time to start!

ADVICE TO YOUNG AND OLD

This advice is for both young and older readers.

Throughout our lives we have practiced getting ready – ready for mealtime, bedtime, school, church, Christmas, etc.

Some folks are always ready and some, seldom.

Some are ready for old age. Most of us are not. Never before have we known what it is like to feel old. I know, because I am old. In some ways I was prepared. In other ways I could have done much better.

But this page is about you. What do I recommend? Recognize that Satan will never stop trying to discourage you. The older we get the harder he will try. He knows that we will soon be transferred to a place where he can never have even a slight hope of decreasing our faith in God. And so he whispers whatever he thinks will influence us.

Jesus had fasted for forty days when Satan appeared on the scene:

Then Satan tempted him to get food by changing stones into loaves of bread. "It will prove you are the Son of God," he said. (Matthew 4:3)

Satan knew Jesus was hungry so he used that to strengthen his attack. Jesus answered him:

"No! For the Scriptures tell us that bread won't feed men's souls: obedience to every word of God is what we need." (Matthew 4:4)

If you haven't started, begin now to be thankful that you are victorious in Christ regardless of what temptation comes to you. When you feel discouraged, God wants you to rejoice. He wants you to sing and make melody in your heart. Satan may whisper, "But you don't feel like it." Know that if you don't feel like it, then that is the time you need to rejoice!

When you hurt or are in poor health, Satan may whisper, "Why doesn't God heal you?" My answer is, "Why did you cause me to be sick?" And then I practice doing what God tells us to do:

Rejoice in the Lord always. (Philippians 4:4 KJV)

Rejoicing opens our hearts to God's peace and joy, which He uses to help us grow in faith. We need faith in God's words so we can use them when we are tired or weary. Faith helps us prepare for times of testing. My advice to you is, be ready!

BACK TO THE BEGINNING

In the beginning, God created Adam and Eve and He said to them:

You must not eat from the tree of the knowledge of good and evil, for when you eat of it you will surely die. (Genesis 2:17 NIV)

Satan countered:

You'll not die! (Genesis 3:4)

They did eat, and they did die – spiritually, and later physically. And they passed on to their children the curse that they had brought upon themselves.

They had separated themselves from God.

Since then, some men have had the faith to believe what God told them:

And Abram believed God; then God considered him righteous on account of his faith. (Genesis 15:6)

Note that God considered Abram righteous because he believed what God told him.

Then there was Joseph. Joseph's brothers had sold him into slavery. In Egypt, Joseph had some good and some very bad times. He was elevated to a high position in the Egyptian government. Years later his brothers came to Egypt to beg for food. Not recognizing Joseph, they stood before him knowing that they were completely at his mercy. Joseph revealed himself to them and said:

As far as I am concerned, God turned into good what you meant for evil, for he brought me to this high position I have today so that I could save the lives of many people. (Genesis 50:20)

Joseph trusted God when everything seemed to be working against him. When nothing seemed to be working for his good he still had faith.

When we believe God's promise to give us eternal life, there may be times when it seems as if there is no way that God would take a miserable person like ourselves to Heaven. That is our opportunity to believe what He has told us over and over again in His Word. Zacharias, the father of John the Baptist, said:

He is sending us a Mighty Savior from the royal line of his servant David, just as he promised through his holy prophets long ago . . .

Making us holy and acceptable, ready to stand in his presence forever . . .

You will tell his people how to find salvation through forgiveness of their sins. All this will be because the mercy of our God is very tender, and heaven's dawn is about to break upon us. (Luke 1:69-70, 75, 77-78)

Long ago God promised to make those who believe Him holy, acceptable, and ready to stand in His presence. He promised salvation and forgiveness of sins. What amazing promises! Yet they are so unlike the way we humans think, making it difficult for us to believe them.

The more I study what God has promised, the more I realize the depth of God's mercy, and I grow to love Him more.

FOREVER IS A LONG TIME

The Lord loves justice and fairness; he will never abandon his people. They will be kept safe forever. (Psalms 37:28)

Forever is a long time.

There are so many things that bring us stress. We can be upset while driving a car. We can be upset at home or at work. At the time, we think that our anger or our impatience is perfectly natural. Yes, it may be natural, but we have the opportunity to be supernatural. We can believe that other people are where they are supposed to be in order to help us learn what we are supposed to learn!

God promises to use every incident and

every circumstance to work for our good. Does this sound too good to be true? Many people have believed Him and are enjoying the benefits of His promise. Only He can do this and it's up to us to believe His promise.

WHAT LIES BEYOND EVERYTHING?

What knowledge do we have of what lies beyond everything we can see with our eyes? Educated men were once quite positive about the size of our universe. They "knew" how many stars there were and how far they were from us. They would have laughed at anyone who believed that there were invisible worlds trillions of miles from earth.

Now astronomers believe that there is space and more space, trillions of miles from earth, filled with elements that are too vast for men to even imagine. The last declarations I saw from astronomers were that there are objects 9,000 light years away from our earth. How far would that be? It is 186,000 miles per second times 9,000 years. There are no numbers to describe such distance.

If men believe such facts about the universe, how could they possibly believe that Heaven is *impossible*? Well-educated scientists now believe in many things they once considered impossible!

Christians can easily believe that it takes less faith to believe what Jesus taught us than it takes to believe that the universe stretches out into eternity. Jesus said we could live forever. We believe Him and we know that He created *whatever is*.

GOD'S SPECIAL SERVANTS

God's special servants carefully explained His plan to bring us to Heaven. If we try to substitute our own plan, as many men have attempted to do, we will be disappointed.

Jesus spoke harshly to spiritual leaders who had devised their own plan of how to please God. They invented laws and threatened punishment to anyone who disobeyed them. They urged everyone to believe that Jesus was leading them into a false religion.

Jeremiah described the terrible condition that he saw:

Listen, O foolish, senseless people – you with the eyes that do not see and the ears that do not listen. (Jeremiah 5:21)

Jeremiah was one of God's special servants. He wrote:

The Lord says: Let not the wise man bask in his wisdom, nor the mighty man in his might, nor the rich man in his riches. Let them boast in this alone: That they truly know me, and understand that I am the Lord of justice and of righteousness whose love is steadfast; and that I love to be this way. (Jeremiah 9:23-24)

God's love for us is steadfast and He enjoys being that way. He is the God represented by the father of the Prodigal Son. This father ran to meet the son who was coming back to him. God runs to meet you and me whenever we come toward Him! He doesn't remind us of our failures when He sees that we want to be forgiven.

If you are unsure whether or not you are going to Heaven, you have the same problem that many people face. Each of us is aware that we could be a better person. We could love God and people more than we do. But we were born with a natural desire to do what we want to do. We may hear the tempter whisper, "If you really were a Christian you would not be the person you are."

God condemns our sins but He loves us and wants to help us receive His forgiveness. That's what He said to us through His special servants.

THE WEDDING FEAST

Jesus gave us the parable of the wedding feast. A king sent invitations to those he wanted at the wedding. But on the day of the wedding everyone the king had invited elected to do something else. They felt justified in their decisions. They had their reasons, but the king did not accept them. So he extended the invitation to others:

Now go out to the street corners and invite everyone you see. (Matthew 22:9)

Among the attendees was a man who did not wear the wedding garment given to him. When asked why he was not wearing the correct garment the man had no excuse:

Then the king said to his aides, "Bind him hand and foot and throw him out into the outer darkness where there is weeping and gnashing of teeth." (Matthew 22:13)

Jesus wanted us to understand that His invitation to receive eternal life has a requirement. Since His invitation is open to everyone, we should not think that God would keep us out of Heaven because we have sinned. Nor should we place our hope in anything good that we do. If we do that we will eventually cause another person to believe the same thing.

Certainly God will not fail to reward the good that we do, but first we must become part of the wedding party and wear the garment He has provided.

NOT INTELLECTUAL ACCEPTANCE

Jesus showed us how important faith is. Faith is not an intellectual acceptance. It is knowing! To one woman Jesus said:

"Daughter, your faith has made you well; go in peace, healed of your disease." (Mark 5:34)

Jesus often spoke similar words; not because a person said, "I believe," but because He knew the person believed. Jesus healed those who believed Him. We may think that believing is not as important as what we do, but the entire Bible emphasizes God's requirement that we have faith in Him. Faith works miracles!

Children obey or disobey based on what they believe will happen as a result. We say, "If you do that again you will be very sorry!" They will obey if they believe what we have told them. Jesus said:

I tell you as seriously as I know how that anyone who refuses to come to God as a little child will never be allowed into his Kingdom. (Mark 10:15)

If children have faith in their parents they believe what they are told.

You and I have been invited to receive the free gift of eternal life, but we must decide if we believe what our Father has told us. When we believe Him we want to tell others what we know. Jesus said to His followers:

You are to go into all the world and preach the Good News to everyone, everywhere. (Mark 16:15)

When we believe what Jesus said about His Good News, we are ready and inspired to convince others.

ACKNOWLEDGE ME

If anyone publicly acknowledges me as his friend, I will openly acknowledge him as my friend before my father in heaven. (Matthew 10:32)

This does not mean we are to acknowledge one time!

We must believe and practice what Jesus told us to do. He taught us to tell His Good News to all the world. To do this effectively we must believe that He will acknowledge us before His Father. When will He do so? When we "publicly acknowledge" Him. That's why I respond as I do when people say, "How are you today?" I may say, "If I were any happier I would have to be in Heaven! That is my great opportunity to openly acknowledge Him!"

Your words now reflect your fate then: either you will be justified by them or you will be condemned. (Matthew 12:37)

Another promise Jesus gave us does not

specifically deal with salvation, but it gives us clear guidance as to what God requires:

If you believe, you will receive whatever you ask for in prayer. (Matthew 21:22 NIV)

If I ask you, "Are you going to Heaven?" and you say, "I'm not sure," what is your status? Either you have not asked God to give you eternal life, or you did ask Him and you do not believe He kept His promise to you.

The most important gift that God has ever given anyone is eternal life. He chose to give this free gift, but we can only receive what we believe. Once we believe what Jesus has said we are called to acknowledge Him before the world. If we do, He promises to acknowledge us before His Father.

LIFETIME OF EXPERIENCE

Jesus told Peter to place his fishing net back in the water. This may have been Peter's first encounter with Jesus.

Peter saw no evidence that they might catch fish since they had been fishing all night and had caught nothing. He probably knew that Jesus was not a fisherman, but Peter decided to trust Jesus rather than what a lifetime of experience had taught him. He let down the fishing net:

And this time their nets were so full that

they began to tear! A shout for help brought their partners in the other boat and soon both boats were filled with fish and on the verge of sinking. When Simon Peter realized what had happened, he fell to his knees before Jesus and said, "Oh, sir, please leave us – I'm too much of a sinner for you to have around." (Luke 5:6-8)

We too have had a lifetime of experience. We know that we make many mistakes and that in God's sight we are far from holy. If we believe that the only way we can make it to Heaven is to become a better person, it may seem wrong for us to declare that we believe we are. But Jesus told us that the only way we can make it is by being perfectly holy. We must place our hope and faith in Him. He said:

I am the Way – yes, and the Truth and the Life. No one can get to the Father except by means of me. (John 14:6)

We must decide if we want to place our confidence in our own qualifications or in what Jesus tells us. Once we decide that we trust in Him to forgive all our sins we feel as Peter did. He said:

We worked hard all last night and didn't catch a thing. But if you say so, we'll try again. (Luke 5:5)

You may have tried to believe that you are a born again child of God, but have repeatedly lost your faith. Now is the time to tell Him, "Jesus, I believe You have done for me what I could not do for myself."

YOUNG GIRL RESURRECTED

A man named Jairus came to plead with Jesus to heal his young daughter. But a messenger from the man's home arrived and told Jairus that his daughter had died. When Jesus heard what had happened He told the father:

Don't be afraid! Just trust me, and she'll be all right. (Luke 8:50)

When Jesus reached the man's home everyone was weeping, but He said:

"Stop the weeping! She isn't dead; she is only asleep!" (Luke 8:52)

Everyone just laughed because they knew the girl was dead.

You may have situations in which you know there is no solution. If urged to have faith you may feel like that will not solve your problem. Jesus demonstrated what He could do:

Then He took her by the hand and called, "Get up, little girl!" And at that moment her life returned and she jumped up! (Luke 8:54-55)

If that were your child would you find it difficult to believe that there is miraculous power in faith?

Our problems may seem too difficult for us to believe that Jesus will solve them. We know that we do not have that kind of faith. We need to learn how to believe! We can only learn by beginning to learn.

The best way to learn is by believing that Jesus does for us exactly what He promises to do. He promises to give us eternal life if we believe Him. People may laugh at us for believing in such a miracle but what greater miracle could we ever receive? Hear His words:

Your names are written in Heaven. (Luke 10:20 NIV)

The Living Translation emphasizes His statement even more clearly:

Your names are registered as citizens of heaven. (Luke 10:20)

How much clearer could Jesus have been? Is He correct, or is Satan correct when he whispers, "But maybe you aren't good enough."

Jesus also said:

I, the Messiah, will publicly honor you in the presence of God's angels if you publicly acknowledge me here on earth as your Friend. (Luke 12:8)

He asks us to publicly acknowledge that He gives us eternal life!

SEVEN TIMES A DAY

Jesus told us to forgive others when they mistreat us.

Even if he wrongs you seven times a day and each time turns again and asks forgiveness, forgive him. (Luke 17:4)

Since Jesus asks us to forgive someone seven times in one day, dare we doubt that He will forgive us many more times in one day? We can surely expect Satan to whisper, "He has not forgiven you."

The law was given by Moses, but grace and truth came by Jesus Christ. (John 1:17 KJV)

God's grace (unmerited favor) was revealed to us by Jesus. Now we know that God wants to forgive us. **To forgive is His nature.** Doubting God seems to be our nature!

You have seen, felt and heard of so many evil things that you may wonder if God is willing to solve everyone's problems. I bear witness that God took my stubborn, rebellious, selfish heart and created in me a desire to please Him, help people, and to tell the world that God loves us. Jesus came:

That all men through him might believe. (John 1:7 KJV)

Jesus gave us the opportunity to believe God. Now we can believe that we are His children, forgiven of all our sins. We should remember that Satan is always whispering,

"But not you." Jesus said of Satan:

He was a murderer from the beginning and a hater of truth – there is not an iota of truth in him. When he lies, it is perfectly normal; for he is the father of liars. (John 8:44)

Satan may hide from you but Jesus knew he was real.

Satan wants us to deny the wonderful Good News that Jesus brought to us. God wants to give us His free gift of eternal life if we will only believe that He wants to forgive us – even seventy times seven in one day.

BORN AGAIN

The words "I have been born again" were once the standard testimony of Christians. Because of our weakness we have permitted those words to become uncommon and even distasteful in Christian circles. We need to frequently review what Jesus said:

With all the earnestness I possess I tell you this: Unless you are born again, you can never get into the Kingdom of God. (John 3:3)

One listener did not understand Jesus' words, and probably many have wanted to ask the same question:

Born again! . . . What do you mean? How can an old man go back into his mother's womb and be born again? (John 3:4)

Jesus' response was:

What I am telling you so earnestly is this: Unless one is born of water and the Spirit, he cannot enter the Kingdom of God. Men can only reproduce human life, but the Holy Spirit gives new life from heaven. (John 3:5-6).

New life in us!

If you have been born again, please join the believing ones who freely proclaim, "I have been born again!" God will never condemn us for believing what Jesus told us. We should believe that "the Holy Spirit" gives "*new life* from heaven" if we want the joy that comes from Heaven.

EATING OUR WAY TO HEAVEN

I am the true Bread from heaven; and anyone who eats this Bread shall live forever. (John 6:58)

Why did God give us such a promise as this? Jesus told us:

You will know the truth, and the truth will set you free. (John 8:32)

It is our God given right to say, "I am free." But Satan whispers, "Doesn't the Bible say that you are a slave to sin?" Yes, it does, but read what else it says:

Slaves don't have rights, but the Son has every right there is! So if the Son sets you free, you will indeed be free. (John 8:35-36)

You do not need to repeatedly tell God that you are a sinner. He is well aware of that. The question is, do you trust Him?

There is no eternal doom awaiting those who trust him to save them. But those who don't trust him have already been tried and condemned for not believing in the only Son of God. (John 3:18)

God speaks to us through His Word in many ways so that there will be no reason for us misunderstanding His plan. But if we do not know what He said we live in bondage to what His enemy keeps saying to us. Once we begin listening to the voice of the Holy Spirit we are able to comprehend what Jesus said to His disciples:

When the Holy Spirit, who is truth, comes, he shall guide you into all truth. (John 16:13)

We do not immediately know everything! But the Holy Spirit will guide us as we learn to listen and let Him guide us into this truth:

I am the true Bread from heaven; and anyone who eats this Bread shall live forever. (John 6:58)

Forever!

If you do not understand how the Father, Son and Holy Spirit work together think of turning the key on a car. The key causes the starter to turn. The starter causes the engine to turn. The engine causes the wheels to turn. But you must first turn the key. You must believe!

REAL FREEDOM

If the Son sets you free, you will indeed be free. (John 8:36)

If you are uncertain what will happen when you die, you will find certainty when you believe that Jesus has set you free from the penalties of all your sins and failures. This is the power that God wants to release in us. This power gives us a greater desire to tell others! Then we understand why Christians have given their lives to help people know Jesus as the One who sets us free, indeed.

They were not executed because they believed in Jesus but because they tried to help other people to believe.

Jesus tells us:

I say emphatically that anyone who listens to my message and believes in God who sent me has eternal life, and will never be damned for his sins, but has already passed out of death into life. (John 5:24)

And He also tells us:

I am the Bread of Life. No one coming to me will ever be hungry again. Those believing in me will never thirst. (John 6:35)

No longer counting on being saved by being

good enough or by obeying God's laws, but by trusting Christ to save me; for God's way of making us right with himself depends on faith – counting on Christ alone. (Philippians 3:9)

NEVER REJECTED

When children disobey their parents they are often punished, but does the parent stop loving them or disown them? No! Parents remain parents through good times and bad.

Jesus wants us to understand that when we believe in Him we have assurance that we are adopted into His family. We remain part of His family during our good times as well as our bad times. Yes, there will come times when we feel as if God is not hearing or answering our prayers. Those are our difficult times. But faith tells us that He is hearing our prayers and will eventually reveal His never-ending love for us. Hear these powerful words from Jesus:

Some will come to me . . . and I will never, never reject them. (John 6:37)

Never, never. What a promise He gives us! This is a promise we should claim no matter how difficult our lives may be. If we cannot believe what Jesus tells us, who then can we believe?

Please see if you can hear Him speak these words:

How earnestly I tell you this - anyone who believes in me already has eternal life! (John 6:47)

Center your thoughts on His use of the words, "eternal life."

He continues to emphasize this point:

I am that Living Bread that came down out of heaven. Anyone eating this Bread shall live forever; this Bread is my flesh given to redeem humanity. (John 6:51)

Listen . . . and believe that this is what He is telling *you.*

GOD PROMISED

Jesus told His disciples:

In just a little while I will be gone from the world, but I will still be present with you. For I will live again – and you will too. (John 14:19)

I believe I will live with Jesus forever! I hope you believe that too.

While I'm spending my last years here on earth I might as well keep enjoying His promise – even though others choose to be unsure of what their future holds.

I recommend that you claim every promise that God offers you. One thing I love to claim is His peace. At one time I would grow restless when I knew that there were many things that needed to be done. Well, some may think, we should be concerned if we have things that need to be done. It all depends on what it is we feel needs to be done. Jesus said that we could have peace:

I am leaving you with a gift – peace of mind and heart! And the peace I give isn't fragile like the peace the world gives. So don't be troubled or afraid. (John 14:27)

So why not enjoy the peace that Jesus wants to give us? When He was here He may have thought of millions of things that He could do. After all, He could do anything! Yet at times He was led to go to a quiet place to rest and pray. God knows that we need time to rest and pray!

Satan tells us differently. He urged Jesus to do things that would prove His faith in God. But Jesus would not accept Satan's ideas. Rather, He chose not to be troubled.

Satan does not want you to believe that you are a child of God because that might lead you to believe that you too could have His peace. You might then believe that you have no need for your heart to be troubled or afraid.

Satan wants us to be unsure of what God has done for us. Otherwise we might be so excited about being a Christian that we would want everyone to have the same joy!

HAVING CHRIST'S JOY

Jesus looked to the heavens and spoke to God:

And now I am coming to You. I have told them many things while I was with them so that they would be filled with my joy. I have given them your commands. And the world hates them because they don't fit in with it, just as I don't. I'm not asking you to take them out of the world, but to keep them safe from Satan's power. (John 17:13-15)

We have the opportunity to have Christ's joy. What potential we have! We could spend all of our time thinking about our own plans and goals, or we could spend time learning how to understand the message Jesus came to give us.

Jesus had such confidence in God's care that He was willing to be hated and despised by men, hang on a cross, and suffer the penalty for our sins. He trusted in God's promise to resurrect Him from the grave.

God did!

And then He ascended into Heaven, watched by many people who told us exactly what they saw. They too were arrested, tortured and killed because they insisted on telling everyone what they had seen and heard.

You and I might one day suffer terrible

persecution, but for now we may face nothing more than ridicule for our faith in what Jesus does for us. If we get His news to others, His joy will increase in us.

Maybe you could get this book to many people.

PROMISES FOR ETERNITY

Yesterday I attended a men's meeting where I was asked to share some of the things I had experienced. When I was finished one man asked me what I was doing now. My immediate response was, "I'm getting happier every day."

Today I'm meditating on why I feel that way. The best explanation I can give is the ever-increasing joy I have. Some folks grieve over getting old. I think it is the best thing that has ever happened to me. My expectations for eternity keep increasing as I meditate on the promises that Jesus gives us. He so clearly explained what His purpose was in coming to this earth. He had such an absolutely clear message to give us. Consider this:

My sheep recognize my voice, and I know them, and they follow me. I give them eternal life and they shall never perish. No one shall snatch them away from me, for my Father has given them to me, and he is more powerful than anyone else, so no one can kidnap them from me. (John 10:27-29)

Those verses cause me to laugh and sing. No power can take me out of God's hand! For all eternity I will have the joy of becoming better acquainted with the Almighty God who created the universe yet is interested in protecting me from any evil that should try to defeat me. When Jesus won the victory over Satan He gave that victory to you and me! The only thing He required of us is that we receive the amazing power of faith. How could we doubt someone who so freely came to suffer and give His life for us?

My upcoming departure from this earth gives me joy as I think about it. I will be able to see Jesus face to face and tell him how thankful I am. It sure seems right to me that I should thank Him now.

I will continue to believe what He told Martha:

I am the one who raises the dead and gives them life again. Anyone who believes in me, even though he dies like anyone else, shall live again. He is given eternal life for believing in me and shall never perish. (John 11:25-26)

Throughout history many men have promised to come back to life. One man kept that promise. **Jesus**.

FOR MEN AND WOMEN

What causes terrible suffering across our country yet is seldom recognized as a problem? This misery visits nearly every family in some way. It overcomes the poor, the rich, the uneducated, the university graduates, and even those who try to live good lives.

This suffering is caused by a desire that lurks within many of us. It is a desire to entertain immoral thoughts. These thoughts often turn into actions. Actions result in divorce, disease, unwanted children, poverty... and the list could go on and on.

Every Christian who entertains immoral thoughts feels the pangs of guilt. Endless prayers are made asking for God's forgiveness. Yet few people seem to know that God has given us the solution to such problems in His Word:

Last of all I want to remind you that your strength must come from the Lord's mighty power within you. Put on all of God's armor so that you will be able to stand safe against all strategies and tricks of Satan. (Ephesians 6:10-11)

Satan's tricks are so destructive! We must put on all of God's armor to stand safe against them. Note that this is something we must do! We can sincerely want God's power to resist evil temptations, but we must also do something. We can spend a lifetime wanting God's help yet consistently fail to do what will help us. The enemy we are fighting is ruthless. He will do anything that he knows will bring suffering to sinners and saints:

For we are not fighting against people made of flesh and blood, but against persons without bodies – the evil rulers of the unseen world, those mighty satanic beings and great evil princes of darkness who rule this world; and against huge numbers of wicked spirits in the spirit world. (Ephesians 6:12)

These forces have great power.

Once again I repeat, there is something we can do:

In every battle you will need faith as your shield to stop the fiery arrows aimed at you by Satan. (Ephesians 6:16)

Men, remember what Jesus says to you:

Anyone who even looks at a woman with lust in his eye has already committed adultery with her in his heart. (Matthew 5:28)

Our excuses are meaningless if we have not done what we can to defeat the fiery arrows aimed at us. But what can we do? The answer is not complicated.

Jesus taught us to pray for one another. That is a simple plan that need not confuse any man or woman. Whenever we see a person who is sexually attractive to us we can begin to pray – not for ourselves but **for**

them. "Help them" prayers are nearly always more powerful than "help me" prayers!

Fix your thoughts on what is true and good and right. Think about things that are pure and lovely, and dwell on the fine, good things in others. Think about all you can praise God for and be glad about. (Philippians 4:8)

We men can pray that God will help that attractive woman, whom God designed, to be the person He wants her to be. We can pray that she will be a godly wife and mother, and be used to win many people to Jesus. We can ask the Holy Spirit to guide our prayers and use them to accomplish things that God wants to do in that beautiful woman. Satan's fiery arrows are turned against him! Our hearts will be blessed. Our joy will increase. We will have a new understanding of the power that God has given us as His children. With this victory our faith will increase and we will have new evidence that we can believe what Jesus tells us. Tears of joy are in my eyes as I remember the times I have said such prayers.

Since I learned to practice this means of serving God my joy has steadily increased. I sense the power that God has given us to experience what Jesus promised:

Happy are those whose hearts are pure, for they shall see God. (Matthew 5:8)

Ladies, please do your best to encourage

every man or boy that you know to read this daily reading book, especially the above section. Most men do not know this power that God has given them.

IMMORAL THOUGHTS

But remember this – the wrong desires that come into your life aren't anything new and different. Many others have faced exactly the same problems before you. And no temptation is irresistible. You can trust God to keep the temptation from becoming so strong that you can't stand up against it, for he has promised this and will do what he says. He will show you how to escape temptation's power so that you can bear up patiently against it. (1 Corinthians 10:13)

We may be ashamed to admit the temptations that come into our minds. We may think of ourselves, as being so weak that God could not love us exactly as we are. But according to this scripture God has a different understanding. He knows millions of men and women who have the same temptations. They too sometimes fail to be the person they want to be.

Humans have forever faced the temptation to think immoral thoughts. You may have struggled with this for years. You may even have reached the point where you think there is no possible way for you to defeat the temptation.

We should not misjudge the seriousness of immoral thoughts. Our natural mind does not always grasp why God is so unhappy with adultery. In the Old Testament He at times struck adulterers dead. That is serious punishment! Why would He do this? That is the wrong question. The right question is, "Why do we not recognize His judgment and do our very best to obey?" Many men and women decide that they are incapable of having thoughts that will please God. Not a good decision.

First, we need to decide what thoughts God hates.

Consider what thoughts you would not want your spouse, mother or pastor to know about. What thoughts do you have that you would not want displayed on a movie screen in your church? If you recognize what thoughts you would be ashamed of, then you can seek to address those thoughts.

Is there a way? God says He will show you "*how to escape.*" All we need to do is to find out how to have the *miracle working power of faith*! But, you may think, I have tried to find that way for many years and I still keep thinking the same thoughts.

It has taken many years for you to develop

the way you think. Your mind follows the same pattern every time you see an attractive temptation. But God says there is an escape.

Here is one of His methods: we can develop a new way of thinking. For example, when you see a woman who attracts your attention, form a new habit. Immediately think something that you believe God would approve of and that you would not be ashamed of. You could think, "Thank you God for creating her and that she is Yours." The prayers you could pray are too numerous to list. Does that mean that at your early attempts to resist temptation you will always be successful? Not necessarily. That will depend on how long you have trained yourself to think immoral thoughts. But if you persist you will soon find many ways to cause Satan to flee. Eventually the first thought that pops into your mind will be one that will cause your heart to rejoice. Your faith will have made a wonderful step forward. Then you will identify other thoughts that have tempted you, and you will be able to escape from those as well. You will rejoice in the way your faith causes you to be increasingly victorious.

FORGIVENESS FOR THE WEAK

Jesus saw the turmoil that was in Peter. He knew Peter would lie and say he did not even know who Jesus was. But Jesus knew the man Peter could become, and He knew that Peter's faith could soon be so strong that he would not deny Jesus even when it meant he too would be tortured and killed.

When Peter was still weak Jesus said to him:

Satan has asked to have you, to sift you like wheat, but I have pleaded in prayer for you that your faith should not completely fail. So when you have repented and turned to me again, strengthen and build up the faith of your brothers. (Luke 22:31-32)

Peter found the miraculous power of faith!

Do you have spiritual strength? If not, now is the time to grow just as Peter did! You can. This book suggests many ways to do so. You can decide, right now, to receive and use the strength that God wants to give every believer.

Did you know that Jesus also prayed for you?

I am not praying for these alone but also for the future believers who will come to me because of the testimony of these. (John 17:20)

Jesus not only prayed for you, He gave His

life for you. He was willing to give everything He had just to help you believe and trust in Him. He knew that was the only way God could accept you as His child.

Jesus knew of the sins His disciples were going to commit yet He promised them a place in Heaven. He told Peter that he would be forgiven of sins that Peter believed he would never commit. You and I are also guilty of sins against God, but God offers forgiveness through Jesus.

A thief on a cross beside Jesus wanted to be forgiven:

He said, "Jesus, remember me when you come into your Kingdom." (Luke 23:42)

Jesus knew his heart and said:

Today you will be with me in Paradise. (Luke 23:43)

Do you believe that God keeps His promise to forgive anyone who trusts in His Son?

THE REALITY OF FORGIVENESS

Jesus said to Paul:

I am going to send you to the Gentiles to open their eyes to their true condition so that they may repent and live in the light of God instead of in Satan's darkness, so that they may receive forgiveness for their sins. (Acts 26:17-18)

It is possible for us to see what is in front of our eyes but be blind to the reality of what we see. God used Paul as a messenger to those who had been so blinded by Satan that they could not receive forgiveness for their sins.

We can ask God to forgive our sins but we must also learn to receive His forgiveness. Why is it that we ask but do not receive? How could that be? To be forgiven we must follow God's instructions. We must believe in our hearts that He does forgive us. We must believe that **He does what only He can do!**

Our innermost being responds to what we believe, not to what we intellectually accept. Believing echoes throughout our entire body! It shines in our eyes! It changes the way we talk about God's goodness and our love for Him.

A lie detector detects when a lie is told, just as our spirit detects when we are not being honest about what we believe. Jesus looked at men and could tell if they believed Him. In some wonderful way our faith reveals itself to Him. God sees our faith and our desire to have faith. I pray that reading this book will help you to believe Him and help others to **know what they know**.

EVERYONE

And all the prophets have written about him, saying that everyone who believes in him will have their sins forgiven through his name. (Acts 10:43)

Here God explained the way He would redeem His creation. Everyone who believes in Jesus will receive forgiveness:

Everyone who trusts in him is freed from all guilt and declared righteous. (Acts 13:39)

Every time I read the word "everyone" my heart sings. I am part of that "everyone" because I trust in Him! The more I read these promises, the stronger my faith becomes. I'm praying that you will be one of those who choose to be freed from all guilt and declared righteous.

Are you going to Heaven? If you have difficulty believing God's promise, now would be a perfect time to answer that question with a great big "Yes!" Then help others to answer, "Yes!"

GOD'S MESSAGE

Paul believed what God told him. He knew that the message he had heard from God would not be well received by the Jews, but he was not ashamed or afraid to tell them. He knew that God had told him the very heart of what the Good News is:

For I am not ashamed of this Good News about Christ. It is God's powerful method of bringing all who believe it to heaven. This message was preached first to the Jews alone, but now everyone is invited to come to God in this same way. (Romans 1:16)

Paul went on to explain the role of faith:

This Good News tells us that God makes us ready for heaven – makes us right in God's sight – when we put our faith and trust in Christ to save us. This is accomplished from start to finish by faith. As the Scripture says it, "The man who finds life will find it through trusting God." (Romans 1:17)

If even one person were taken to Heaven because of his or her own goodness, God would be proven to be a liar! That will never happen. Paul amplified this point when he said:

There is no one righteous, not even one. (Romans 3:10 NIV)

God knew that some people in Paul's generation would not believe His Good News but He instructed Paul to continue preaching His important message:

But now God has shown us a different way to heaven – not by "being good enough" and trying to keep his laws, but by a new way (though not new, really, for the Scriptures told about it long ago). Now God says he will accept and acquit us – declare us "not guilty" – if we trust Jesus Christ to take away our sins. And we all can be saved in this same way, by coming to Christ, no matter who we are or what we have been like. Yes, all have sinned; all fall short of God's glorious ideal; yet now God declares us "not guilty" of offending him if we trust in Jesus Christ, who in his kindness freely takes away our sins.

For God sent Christ Jesus to take the punishment for our sins and to end all God's anger against us. He used Christ's blood and our faith as the means of saving us from his wrath. (Romans 3:21-25)

WHAT CAN WE BOAST ABOUT?

What can we boast about doing, to earn our salvation? Nothing at all. Why? Because our acquittal is not based on our good deeds; it is based on what Christ has done and our faith in him. So it is that we are saved by faith in Christ and not by the good things we do. (Romans 3:27-28)

Christ has done it all. We just believe in what He has done. He did what we could never do:

Yes, all have sinned; all fall short of God's glorious ideal; yet now God declares us "not guilty" of offending him if we trust in Jesus Christ, who in his kindness freely takes away our sins. (Romans 3:23)

That verse says all have sinned, but it also gives a wonderful promise for those who have come to Christ. They are not guilty. Only God could make such a powerful declaration. Our salvation is not based on our good deeds but now upon:

    1. What Christ has done.

    2. Our faith in Him.

This gives us reason to rejoice!

IF WE PAY ATTENTION

When we pay attention we become increasing aware that Satan is always contradicting what God says. He has been following this method since he first spoke to Adam and Eve. He knows that God gives us a desire to do good things so he preys on our failures. He may cause us to feel proud that we are doing good things, or to feel bad that we are doing wrong things. His purpose is still the same. He wants to steer us away from believing that God wants to forgive us.

Paul addresses this very subject in the book of Romans. God wants to give us incentives to believe what He says rather than what Satan says:

Being saved is a gift; if a person could earn it by being good, then it wouldn't be free – but it is! It is given to those who do not work for it. For God declares sinners to be good in his sight if they have faith in Christ to save them from God's wrath. (Romans 4:4-5)

Speak those words to yourself and consider the huge blessing that God wants to give you. He gives us warning after warning of the consequences of trying to be good enough to receive eternal life by what we do, or do not do.

REAL PEACE

So now, since we have been made right in God's sight by faith in his promises, we can have real peace with him because of what Jesus Christ our Lord has done for us. (Romans 5:1)

There is more to God's message than His forgiveness of our sins. He wants to demonstrate His love for us.

We must not ignore that:

Adam caused many to be sinners because he disobeyed God, and Christ caused many to be made acceptable to God because he obeyed. (Romans 5:19)

Adam's sin nature was passed on to his children and from them to each generation that followed. Then another man was born,

Jesus Christ. Through faith in Him we can have peace with God!

Consider how you would feel if your son gave his life to save another person's son, and then that family began to claim that they had saved their son by something they did. You would not be happy! God sent His Son to die for us and God will not accept our refusal to believe that because of His Son our names are written in Heaven.

I AM CONVINCED

I am convinced that neither death nor life, neither angels nor demons, neither the present nor the future, nor any powers, neither height nor depth, nor anything else in all creation, will be able to separate us from the love of God that is in Christ Jesus our Lord. (Romans 8:38-39 NIV)

Read those verses several times.

How much clearer could God have been in describing His love for us? What can separate us from God's love? Death, life, angels, demons?

Power is available to us because of our faith in Christ Jesus. The stronger our faith becomes the more we realize what He has done for us. Faith in Jesus protects us – eternally – from everything!

Hear what Jesus said:

My sheep recognize my voice, and I know them, and they follow me. I give them eternal life and they shall never perish. No one shall snatch them away from me, for my Father has given them to me, and he is more powerful than anyone else, so no one can kidnap them from me. (John 10:27-29)

What confidence He wants us to have! Jesus promises that no one can take us away from Him! He knew that Satan would try every trick he knows to prevent us from receiving the eternal life promised to us. Every Christian faces these temptations, but we can resist them.

How can we have the faith to resist?

Faith comes from listening to this Good News – the Good News about Christ. (Romans 10:17)

We need to be so convinced that we will tell others!

For if you tell others with your own mouth that Jesus Christ is your Lord, and believe in your own heart that God has raised him from the dead, you will be saved. For it is by believing in his heart that a man becomes right with God; and with his mouth he tells others of his faith, confirming his salvation. (Romans 10:9-10)

"How are you today? "I'm wonderful because Jesus is my Savior."

God's plan is ever so simple. Believing and telling others strengthens our own faith and helps others to believe. Satan's plan is to keep us quiet because he knows the power in God's plan! That is why Christians will always hear the ugly voice telling them that they are not the "talking type." Remember that God did not call just gifted talkers to tell others. He calls every Christian to tell others. Please mark that down in your head and heart so you will remember it is with your mouth that you tell others of your faith, confirming your salvation.

THE POWER OF FEAR

Christians are tempted to be afraid. There are many ways for our enemy to tempt us. Once a specific fear has taken root in someone's heart it becomes so powerful that the person believes they have no way to overcome it. The word "fear" appears in 385 verses of the Bible! Fear has power over us unless we learn how to overcome it by the power of the Holy Spirit, one step at a time.

First we must have faith that God can and wants to deliver us. Note that Jesus was never afraid. His disciples were afraid at times until they began to understand what Jesus taught them. Before Jesus was crucified Peter was positive that nothing would make him afraid, but when Jesus was arrested Peter soon fell into the temptation that comes to every one of us.

Fear arrives at unexpected times, gains a foothold, and then keeps coming back until we think it is a natural part of our human nature. Babies are unafraid of falling down until they learn that it can be painful. This is a natural learning process. But some children become so fearful that even when they are adults they have a strong, sometimes over-whelming, fear of falling. In the Army I saw men so afraid that they were paralyzed. Other soldiers couldn't understand why these men were so afraid. Usually the man himself could not understand.

There are a multitude of things you may fear, but don't feel defeated. God will help you if you learn to have faith that He will. Remember, faith is miraculous.

You may be afraid of losing your health, wealth, job, friends, or your life. If there is something that you are afraid of, take heart:

Fear not, for I am with you. Do not be dismayed. I am your God. I will strengthen you; I will help you; I will uphold you with my victorious right hand. (Isaiah 41:10)

You may be afraid that you are not righteous enough for God to strengthen you. If so, realize that it is fear itself that causes you to have that thought! The verse says that God upholds us by His righteousness, not ours!

If we firmly believe that and practice praising God for everything, we become increasingly aware that God is always teaching us to have faith in Him.

If you do this you will experience God's peace, which is far more wonderful than the human mind can understand. His peace will keep your thoughts and your hearts quiet and at rest as you trust in Christ Jesus. (Philippians 4:7)

Peace is God's gift that comes through trusting in Christ Jesus!

Jesus is here to help every person who wants to learn how to believe Him. We learn to believe Him by His power, not our power.

BLIND

Satan, the god of this evil world, has blinded the minds of those who don't believe, so they are unable to see the glorious light of the Good News that is shining upon them. They don't understand the message we preach about the glory of Christ. (2 Corinthians 4:4)

Jesus promised us that the Holy Spirit would help us learn things that others would never know.

What we see, hear and feel are fundamentals that our minds use to decide what we think and believe. Jesus kept emphasizing to the disciples that the world they saw was not the world in which He lived. They saw, heard and felt the waves threatening to sink their boat. In Jesus' way of seeing, hearing and feeling, there was no problem. Peter saw the waves, felt the wind, and sank. Jesus saw and was able to take Peter's hand and lift him out of the water. In years to come I wonder how frequently the other disciples wondered, "Why didn't I try to walk on the water?"

Jesus challenges you and me to believe and open our eyes to see that He is with us. Yes, the winds and storms of life will tell us that there is nothing we can do to know we are victorious, that we will never successfully stand upright by faith, or that we cannot see and hear the message that God wants us to have faith in Him. But we can!

When can we do this? Every moment of every day, and in every circumstance. These are the victories that Jesus came to help us receive. Jesus taught His disciples how to have faith in Him and in many ways they learned to be like Him. How can we learn to experience the same victories? One step at a time:

For we walk by faith, not by sight. (2 Corinthians 5:7 KJV)

If we learn to walk by faith in what Jesus taught us, will we someday be disappointed? That depends on whether we learn to grow in faith one step at a time.

Our bodies may hurt or feel tired and weary, but we can learn to hear and believe what Jesus is saying to us: "Walk by faith, not by sight." We can strive to have eyes that are no longer blind and ears that are no longer deaf.

Paul practiced growing in faith and concluded:

No one who believes in Christ will ever be disappointed. (Romans 10:11)

The longer I believe, the stronger my faith grows and the more joy I have in knowing that my name is written in Heaven.

NEW LIFE

When we do not believe what God promises us, it is difficult to grasp what the Bible says. The Bible says this:

Listen, O foolish, senseless people – you with the eyes that do not see and the ears that do not listen. (Jeremiah 5:21)

When we believe what God promises us, something happens:

When someone becomes a Christian he

becomes a brand new person inside. He is not the same any more. A new life has begun! (2 Corinthians 5:17)

We have this new life when we believe that it is a free gift from God. We receive something new. We realize that we are new people. We understand that this is a gift and not because of something we did:

All these new things are from God who brought us back to himself through what Christ Jesus did. (2 Corinthians 5:18)

Over and over the Bible emphasizes that we receive new life because of something God does for us. What a joy it is to know that through what Jesus did, God brought us back to Himself.

When we know that God has saved us through our faith in Jesus we have the joy of telling others that God wants to do the same for them. If someone had heard all their life that they must stop sinning before God will accept them, they may have given up hope of ever becoming a new person.

You can present them with the Good News:

And God has given us the privilege of urging everyone to come into his favor and be reconciled to him. For God was in Christ, restoring the world to Himself, no longer counting men's sins against them but blotting them out. This is the wonderful message he has given us to tell others. (2 Corinthians 5:18-19)

IT CHANGES EVERYTHING

When we believe that Jesus took our sin upon Himself, it changes everything. He did not come to change us so that we would never sin again. That would mean that we would live the same sinless life that He lived. The 12 disciples and the early Christians failed to be like Jesus in many ways! They didn't claim to be perfect. They believed that by faith they had the free gift of eternal life.

We can believe that we are going to Heaven because of what Jesus did for us!

We are by our human nature prone to sin – in many ways – but there is only one thing that will prevent us from going to Heaven: not believing God's promise as recorded in John 3:16 and many other verses. Believing we can go to Heaven if we just become a better person is *the opposite of what Jesus told us*. Our only hope is to be confident in what He did for us.

Is there something we must do in order to receive God's forgiveness? Yes. God made it simple so we have no excuse for not doing what He says:

If we confess our sins to him, he can be depended on to forgive us and to cleanse us from every wrong. (1 John 1:9)

Because of Satan we became sinners. Because of Jesus we can be forgiven!

Having such great promises as these, dear friends, let us turn away from everything wrong, whether of body or spirit, and purify ourselves, living in the wholesome fear of God, giving ourselves to him alone. (2 Corinthians 7:1)

We now want to please God. When we fail to do so we ask Him to forgive us. He does. Paul explains that to us:

God took the sinless Christ and poured into him our sins. Then, in exchange, he poured God's goodness into us! (2 Corinthians 5:21)

Paul begs us to remember what God has done for us:

As God's partners we beg you not to toss aside this marvelous message of God's great kindness. (2 Corinthians 6:1)

By His kindness we receive a new status. He says:

I will live with them and walk among them, and I will be their God and they shall be my people. (2 Corinthians 6:16)

Think of it! We are living with God. He claims us as His people! We can help others realize what God wants to do for them. Satan has convinced many people that God doesn't care about them. But God wants to do great things for them! As we grow in our belief of this truth we want to spread His Good News to every hurting person in the world. We want them to hear His words:

I will welcome you, and be a Father to you, and you will be my sons and daughters. (2 Corinthians 6:17-18)

Today is a good day to do what Paul urged us to do. He wrote:

Check up on yourselves. Are you really Christians? Do you pass the test? Do you feel Christ's presence and power more and more within you? Or are you just pretending to be Christians when actually you aren't at all? (2 Corinthians 13:5)

Have you heard the chorus "Shout unto God with the voice of triumph"? We may feel weak but faith in God's power helps us to claim triumph. We may not feel triumphant but we can remember that we walk by faith, not by what we feel. God calls us to do this because He knows that with faith in Him we can be happy in a very unhappy world.

God sent His Son Jesus so that we could be forgiven and experience everything He promised to those who believe. When we believe that Jesus died for our sins it changes everything! That is the miraculous power in faith!

HAVING PROBLEMS?

This world can give us problems – have you ever noticed? When God planned a way to help us He knew every scheme that Satan would use to create problems. God has known every person since He first created Adam and Eve.

God permits us to make mistakes, but He also provided a way for us to be forgiven. His plan is what we call "the Good News."

May peace and blessing be yours from God the Father and from the Lord Jesus Christ. He died for our sins just as God our Father planned, and rescued us from this evil world in which we live. (Galatians 1:3-4)

God made it possible for us to live in this present evil age and yet be sure we have received His grace. In the verses that follow, Paul uses strong language to describe anyone who distorts this Gospel that Jesus gave us:

For there is no other way than the one we showed you; you are being fooled by those who twist and change the truth concerning Christ. Let God's curses fall on anyone, including myself, who preaches any other way to be saved than the one we told you about; yes, if an angel comes from heaven and preaches any other message, let him be forever cursed. (Galatians 1:7-8)

Paul was disturbed when he saw Peter doing something in Antioch that might hinder Christians from understanding what grace is. So he told Peter that he was doing wrong.

Peter had been eating with the Gentiles. When men who worked with James came to

Antioch, Peter stopped eating with Gentiles. He knew these men might tell James what he was doing. This may seem like a very small thing to us, but Paul did not want God's grace toward those who believe in Jesus to be distorted.

Paul saw that other Jews in Antioch including Barnabas were already following Peter's example, so Paul took action. In a gathering of the church he told Peter that he did not have the right to distort The Gospel:

Convinced that no human being can please God by self-improvement, we believed in Jesus as the Messiah so that we might be set right before God by trusting in the Messiah, not by trying to be good. (Galatians 2:16 MSG)

Having problems? Trust in Jesus.

Elsewhere Paul tells us:

Now we can come fearlessly right into God's presence, assured of his glad welcome when we come with Christ and trust in him. (Ephesians 3:12)

SOMETHING NEW

In the book of Isaiah God emphasizes His desire to do something new and wonderful:

I, yes, I alone am He who blots away your sins for my own sake and will never think of them again. (Isaiah 43:25)

What great news! Isaiah puts it this way:

Oh, the joy of drinking deeply from the Fountain of Salvation! (Isaiah 12:3)

When I asked God to forgive my sins, and believed that He did, I knew nothing about the Fountain of Salvation, but I suddenly knew that I had joy. The old Merlin was gone and I wanted to learn more about God's great salvation. I'm still learning and still drinking His living water.

Throughout the Old Testament men failed to do what God told them to do. But God had a plan. He began to reveal what He would do for us, something new. He would blot out our sins so that He would not think of them again. He would do what we cannot do. If we think we can achieve righteousness by our own efforts we will be declaring that it is not God who blots away our sins.

Sin is harmful to us and to others. Yet it is disguised as something good. In the Garden of Eden sin was portrayed as the best thing men and women could hope for. But it wasn't, and it never is. For example, if we are tempted to eat more than we should, our mind pictures the pleasure as something good. But the results are much different.

Believing in Jesus as our Savior does not mean that from that point on everything will be wonderful. It is then that the process of refinement begins – a process by which we become something new. In Isaiah 48:10 God says:

I refined you in the furnace of affliction.

HEALED

God wants to strengthen our faith and He has many reasons for doing so. The stronger our faith becomes the more He can use us to help others! The problem is, we are sinful.

Men like Isaiah had to go through many difficulties to prepare them for the work God wanted them to do. If we are ready and willing to be changed God will abundantly reward us both in this life and in eternity.

We may not realize how much we need God to change us. Psalm 51:5 tells us what He thinks:

Born a sinner, yes, from the moment my mother conceived me.

The same is true for all of us. That means we were in sin before we were born! Many changes need to happen in us. We need to be healed.

It was for that very reason that God sent His own Son:

He was wounded and bruised for our sins. He was chastised that we might have peace; he was lashed – and we were healed! (Isaiah 53:5)

Why is all of this important? Why is it extremely important? God loved His Son far more than you and I will ever love anyone. Yet He permitted Him to be a sacrifice for our sake. We must believe that Jesus was wounded for our sins so that we could be healed!

God did something extra special for Isaiah. Isaiah received what would one day come to you and me:

Let me tell you how happy God has made me! For he has clothed me with garments of salvation and draped about me the robe of righteousness. I am like a bridegroom in his wedding suit or a bride with her jewels. (Isaiah 61:10)

UNBELIEVABLE

Satan's persistent suggestions can convince us that God is not willing to give us the free gift of His love and grace. Grace means unmerited favor. But our lifelong experience is that nothing is free.

Jesus said to some:

You are slaves of sin, every one of you . . . And yet some of you are trying to kill me because my message does not find a home within your hearts. (John 8:34, 37)

They had heard Jesus, but refused to

believe Him. Still today people hear but refuse to believe that:

Only by his undeserved favor have we ever been saved. (Ephesians 2:5)

To this day there are some who cannot believe that Jesus wants to hand them the keys to Heaven. The height and depth of Jesus' love and power is too marvelous for them to believe. If you have not yet believed in Jesus' power and love, please bow your head and tell Him that you believe and will continue to believe, forever.

CHANGED

When we believe what Jesus taught, the Holy Spirit does His work in us. We then want to tell others what He will do for them. This is what happened to the first Christians:

The same Good News that came to you is going out all over the world and changing lives everywhere, just as it changed yours that very first day you heard it and understood about God's great kindness to sinners. (Colossians 1:6)

What was it about the new message that caused lives to be changed wherever it was preached? The Jewish faith was built on the way people could receive forgiveness for their sins. People were required to repeatedly offer animals to be sacrificed for their sins. But this new Good News said anyone could be forgiven without following the old Jewish rules.

This Good News made it possible for both Jews and Gentiles to be forgiven, no strings attached. Nothing so marvelous had ever been heard of. As people realized the miracle of their changed lives they joyfully told others what had happened to them.

Can you imagine the questions that were asked of these early believers? "You really felt a change in you? In what ways are you different now? Can you explain it to us?" They may have replied, "All I can tell you is that when I believed I became certain that I will go to Heaven."

I can well remember the change that happened in me when I first believed. My life changed. I wanted to please God and to serve Him. Knowing that I was a child of God did something in me that words couldn't easily describe. Almost immediately I wanted to tell people what had happened to me. After sixty-five years I still want to tell people how they can know they are going to Heaven. I under-stood what God had done for me:

He has rescued us out of the darkness and gloom of Satan's kingdom and brought us into the kingdom of his dear Son. (Colossians 1:13)

In 1972 God helped Mary and me to begin

a brand new church here in California. My message centered in salvation by faith in Jesus. Every Sunday many people came forward to receive Jesus as Savior. Now, forty nine years later, I regularly meet or hear from people who say, "I remember that day when I first knew for sure that I was a born again believer in Jesus."

If you are one of those who want to obey God but feel alienated from Him, you can be victorious over Satan's accusations against you. Believe that God has brought you into the kingdom of His Son.

A NEW WAY OF LIVING

For God has not chosen to pour out his anger upon us, but to save us through our Lord Jesus Christ; he died for us so that we can live with him forever. (1 Thessalonians 5:9-10)

If God wanted to He could find many things wrong with us – in our thoughts, desires and actions. But now because of Jesus and our faith in Him, God sees us as covered by His blanket of love! What greater gift could God possibly give us? That is why His angels announced that Jesus' birth was "Good News." Because of this news we are invited into a new way of living that does not depend on our own good deeds. God tells us to:

Always be joyful. Always keep on praying. No matter what happens, always be thankful, for this is God's will for you who belong to Christ Jesus. (1 Thessalonians 5:16-18)

Living this way causes our enemy to take action. He has many reasons why you should not always be joyful and he will tell you what they are. But God wants to assure us that we can be joyful always:

May the God of peace himself make you entirely pure and devoted to God; and may your spirit and soul and body be kept strong and blameless until that day when our Lord Jesus Christ comes back again. (1 Thessalonians 5:23)

Nothing short of God's power could work such a miracle.

GREAT JOY IN CONFIDENCE

Let us then approach the throne of grace with confidence, so that we may receive mercy and find grace to help us in our time of need. (Hebrews 4:16 NIV)

With confidence. How can we have confidence in what will happen to us when we die? The more we believe that Jesus has paid the price for our complete forgiveness and pardon, the more confidence we will have!

The more we search the Bible the more

evidence we find that God has given us many promises. He has made an oath:

God also bound himself with an oath, so that those who received the promise could be perfectly sure that he would never change his mind. (Hebrews 6:17)

We can count on God to keep His promise and His oath:

So God has given us both his promise and his oath. These two things are unchangeable because it is impossible for God to lie. Therefore, we who have fled to him for refuge can take new courage, for we can hold on to his promise with confidence. (Hebrews 6:18)

Reader, if we cannot trust in God's promises we are hopelessly adrift in the vast sea of eternity. Our only hope is to have confidence in the Creator who came to earth and gave His life for us:

This confidence is like a strong and trustworthy anchor for our souls. It leads us through the curtain of heaven into God's inner sanctuary. (Hebrews 6:19)

JESUS LEARNED THROUGH SUFFERING

And even though Jesus was God's Son, he had to learn from experience what it was like to obey, when obeying meant suffering. It was after he had proved himself perfect in this experience that Jesus became the Giver of eternal salvation to all those who obey him. (Hebrews 5:8-9)

Throughout His ministry Jesus repeated one message over and over: have faith in God! His message was valid because He knew what it meant to experience suffering. His disciples repeated His message.

Instead of relying on faith, the religious leaders demanded that everyone honor the law. To them it was more important than anything, and they were willing to kill anyone who failed to honor what they believed was God's holy law.

Jesus' disciples also suffered. They continued teaching what He had taught them, regardless of being stoned, whipped or imprisoned:

Let us stop going over the same old ground again and again, always teaching those first lessons about Christ. Let us go on instead to other things and become mature in our understanding, as strong Christians ought to be. Surely we don't need to speak further about the foolishness of trying to be saved by being good, or about the necessity of faith in God. (Hebrews 6:1)

Now we need to go over the "the same old grounds again and again" because so many people believe they must be better than they are before they could hope to know they are "saved."

OUR LIVING SAVIOR

We are not dependent upon a Savior who is dead. Jesus is alive! He is with God the Father and continues to serve as our Savior.

What if we know Jesus as our Savior but die before we repent of some sin? We still have Jesus as the One who is seated beside God. He intercedes for us. He will not say, "But he is a good person." That is no excuse for our disobedience. Jesus will say that He paid the price for our sin because we believed in Him and trusted in Him:

He is able to save completely all who come to God through him. Since he will live forever, he will always be there to remind God that he has paid for their sins with his blood. (Hebrews 7:25)

What confidence we have in our Savior! This is the message that is called the Good News. This is the message that you and I are called to take to the entire world. The center of this message is the fact that God wants to forgive us:

I will be merciful to them in their wrongdoings, and I will remember their sins no more. (Hebrews 8:12)

OUR PERFECT FATHER

Have you ever tried to imagine a perfect God? The Bible describes Him to us. Some readers may think they know what a perfect God should look like, but a careful study of His Word clearly shows us that our God is more loving and kind than we can imagine.

I've heard people say that they wish God would simply change everyone and make them perfectly holy. Then, in their minds, everything would be perfect forever. But remember that when God created Adam and Eve they were perfect. Since they were created in His image they had the freedom to decide what they wanted to do. If God had created them so that they could only choose good things, they would not have been like Him since He can choose what He wants to do.

So God chose to send His Son to earth with the freedom to do whatever He wanted to do. Jesus lived a perfect life and then gave His life as a gift to us! We don't fully understand this but we can accept His gift if we so choose:

What a God we have! And how fortunate we are to have him, this Father of our Master Jesus! Because Jesus was raised from the dead, we've been given a brand – new life and have everything to live for, including a future in heaven – and the future starts now! (1 Peter 1:3-4 MSG)

I choose Jesus as Master and I have "everything to live for."

OUR GREAT WEALTH

Regardless of how little money we have, we feel wealthy when we realize how valuable our faith is:

Your faith is far more precious to God than mere gold; so if your faith remains strong after being tried in the test tube of fiery trials, it will bring you much praise and glory and honor on the day of his return. (1 Peter 1:7)

We should measure our wealth on God's scales. He knows how valuable faith is. Remember that Jesus had no home and no possessions, yet He could feed thousands of people, turn water into wine, cause fish to swim into fishermen's nets, and raise the dead. Surely we would prefer to have the wealth He had.

Peter gave up everything to follow Jesus. What an honor it would be to know that God had chosen you to be a disciple. We too are highly honored! We are chosen to be God's children! We can walk down the street with the assurance that no matter what people may think, we are special. Both now and in eternity we have access to God whenever we want to talk with Him. What higher honor can anyone ever have? We are told:

O clap your hands, all ye people; shout unto God with the voice of triumph. (Psalms 47:1 KJV)

When I read that verse I feel triumphant – not because of anything I have done but because of what Jesus did for everyone who has faith in Him!

PRAYERS FOR HEALING

I often hear from people who have prayed over and over for some good thing, such as healing for a person they love. They base their faith on passages like this:

And we are sure of this, that He will listen to us whenever we ask him for anything in line with His will. And if we really know He is listening when we talk to Him and make our requests, then we can be sure that He will answer us. (1 John 5:14-15)

The most important part of these verses is the phrase "in line with His will." Have you noticed that people will pray for nearly anything that they want? That's part of our natural attitude. We may want an automobile, or many other things, so we ask God to give us those things. Would these requests be in line with His will? We don't know. Is it always His will to heal us when we are ill? Often when we are hurting we are sure that that is His will. But perhaps God is refining us to better serve Him. We will be rewarded with a perfect new body in Heaven where we will live with Him forever.

When my Grandmother Carothers was dying she suffered intensely, but she wanted to live long enough to tell me something. For many years she believed that God had called me to serve Him in special ways. What she told me during her final hours was not so spectacular that it would have benefited everyone. She simply said, "Merlin, the music. Don't miss it." That meant something special to me. I had often sat beside her during the singing of hymns. She could not sing in tune. Many people told her so but she continued to sing. As she was nearing Heaven God introduced her to how heavenly music sounded. I know that now she is able to sing with the best of them!

My grandmother inspired me to do the best I can and leave the rest to God. That is the way I pray. I pray the best I know how, and leave the rest to God. I recommend that you pray that way. If you do, you will never be tempted to doubt our God who gave His only Son to provide us with the gift of eternal life.

DEFEATING SIN

If we say that we have no sin, we are only fooling ourselves, and refusing to accept the truth. But if we confess our sins to him, he can be depended on to forgive us and to cleanse us from every wrong. And it is perfectly proper for God to do this for us because Christ died to wash away our sins. (1 John 1:8-9)

Every one of us sins. That is why we need Jesus Christ:

Stay away from sin. But if you sin, there is someone to plead for you before the Father. His name is Jesus Christ, the one who is all that is good and who pleases God completely. (1 John 2:1)

No matter how bad our sins may be, God provides a perfect solution. The following verses demonstrate how God solved the entire sin problem that we humans have. He provided what I call His blanket of love. When He looks at us He sees that blanket:

God showed how much he loved us by sending his only Son into this wicked world to bring to us eternal life through his death. In this act we see what real love is: it is not our love for God, but his love for us when he sent his Son to satisfy God's anger against our sins. (1 John 4:9-10)

By His forgiving grace He provided what we could never attain for ourselves. That is

why the early Christian church was so determined to get this Good News to the entire
world. If we want to be excited about Jesus
we must let His Spirit fill our hearts with the
knowledge of *what Jesus has done for us!*

We can be used by God to overcome the
forces that want to destroy every human
being. God's resources are available to us:

*For every child of God can obey him,
defeating sin and evil pleasure by trusting
Christ to help him.* (1 John 5:4)

All the talents that men have ever
possessed could not replace what God can do
through us. By our faith in Him, Jesus said
we could tell mountains to move. But this
book is about receiving God's most important
gift, eternal life through His magnificent gift
of faith. Once faith in Jesus is firmly estab-
lished in our hearts, we know that we have
eternal life:

*All who believe this know in their hearts
that it is true. If anyone doesn't believe this,
he is actually calling God a liar, because he
doesn't believe what God has said about his
Son. And what is it that God has said? That
he has given us eternal life, and that this life
is in his Son.* (1 John 5:10-11)

Call God a liar? Not me!

WHAT JOHN KNEW

John knew that faith in Jesus was the answer to all of our questions about what will happen to us when we die. He emphasized what Christian faith is all about:

I have written this to you who believe in the Son of God so that you may know you have eternal life. (1 John 5:13)

We know! This is quite a statement that Jesus' half-brother wrote. He saw what Jesus had done and he believed what Jesus had said. John believed that he and those who believe in Jesus are God's children.

Children who love their parents are pleased and proud to identify themselves with them. They are not hesitant to claim them as their parents. If you are a child of God you can be proud to say, "God is my Father. And that makes me His child." Once God accepts you as His child He will never say, "You are no longer my child." Yes, He may discipline you just as any loving parent would, but even as you hurt from the discipline, remember who you are!

If our faith in God is so weak that we do not know what we believe about Him, we place ourselves at the mercy of the evil one:

We know that we are children of God and that all the rest of the world around us is under Satan's power and control. (1 John 5:19)

I surely do not want the evil one to have any control over me!

RADIANT FACES

If you are filled with light within, with no dark corners, then your face will be radiant too, as though a floodlight is beamed upon you. (Luke 11:36)

You and I are a reflection of what is in us. We have imperfections, but we can set our sights on what we can become with the help of the Holy Spirit. To do this we must deal with what is already within us. Everything we have done, or thought of doing, is stored in our minds! Those things are part of us. They influence everything we do, even when we are unaware of them. For example, I've noticed that when I walk I always begin with my left foot. Why? Can you guess? Twenty years in the Army. When I try to begin with my right foot it seems strange to me. What I have heard and done influences everything I do – even the writing of these words.

Your thoughts are molding you. If for most of your life you thought that in order to get to Heaven you had to become a certain kind of person, that thought is buried in your mind. If you must, begin new thoughts. Center your attention on the promises you find in this small book. Everything Jesus told us is powerful. Once you grasp the power of His Words you become a new person:

And now – all glory to him who alone is God, who saves us through Jesus Christ our Lord; yes, splendor and majesty, all power and authority are his from the beginning; his they are and his they evermore shall be. And he is able to keep you from slipping and falling away, and to bring you, sinless and perfect, into his glorious presence with mighty shouts of everlasting joy. Amen. (Jude 1:24-25)

The Merlin I know is not "sinless and perfect" but the One who lives in me has given me His sinless perfection as His free gift. I look forward to seeing the new you when we get to Heaven.

DYING

Everyone would like to know that they will die peacefully, but the question many have is, "How can I know in advance?" There is only one way that I know of. We can believe what Jesus taught us. He didn't promise us a painless death, but He did offer to give us the free gift of complete peace concerning the when and how.

Do you know that many people spend years worrying about their coming death?

They have never met anyone who has come back to life so they have no one to explain what will happen at the moment of death.

The Bible tells us about people who were brought back to life, but have you noticed that the Bible does not tell us what they experienced? All we need to know is what Jesus tells us. He died and came back to life in order to confirm all the things He taught us. God wants our faith to be in Jesus as the One who knows the beginning and the end.

Jesus told us:

I am leaving you with a gift – peace of mind and heart! And the peace I give isn't fragile like the peace the world gives. So don't be troubled or afraid. (John 14:27)

This world cannot give us this peace. Jesus can! Anyone who believes they have *peace of mind* because they live a good life, will eventually be *troubled or afraid.* Our faith is in Jesus, not in ourselves.

WHERE IS JESUS?

Where is Jesus right now?

Before Jesus left this earth He promised to live in us:

In just a little while I will be gone from the world, but I will still be present with you. For I will live again – and you will too. When I

come back to life again, you will know that I
am in my Father, and you in me, and I in you.
(John 14:19-20)

As we grow in faith we become increasingly aware of Jesus' presence in us. It's not
that He doesn't want us to be completely
aware of His presence, but He wants us to
grow in faith and not rely on what we see or
feel. During His time on earth He repeatedly
emphasized that what we believe will become
real to us.

When Jesus brought a dead person back
to life He did so because someone had faith
in Him. We have faith that He lives in us and
our faith helps us know that we have been
given a new life. Every experience that we
have is an opportunity for us to believe what
Jesus came to tell us. He said:

*The thief's purpose is to steal, kill and
destroy. My purpose is to give life in all its
fullness.* (John 10:10)

Jesus spent His life giving to anyone who
wanted His help. He still wants to give life in
all its fullness to anyone who will believe Him.

OPEN THE DOOR

*Look! I have been standing at the door and
I am constantly knocking. If anyone hears me
calling him and opens the door, I will come*

in and fellowship with him and he with me.
(Revelation 3:20)

I knew Jesus was knocking at my door and I said, "Yes, Jesus, please come in." He came in. I didn't deserve to have such a One living in me, but He came in just as He had promised.

If you have invited Jesus to live in you, please believe that He has kept His promise. He said, "I will come in."

Don't be hesitant to tell people that He lives in you and has promised to live in you for all eternity! That is Good News. He comes to live in those who know they need Him and in those who are willing to tell others that He keeps His promises.

We need to remember that Satan will use even God's words to accuse us. He wants us to ignore God's promise to forgive all our sins. We need to know and affirm that we are no longer under the hold Satan once had on us.

But Satan still has a hold on some and we need to show them the love of God. Many people today believe in God but not in Jesus. Such persons believe that it is better to have faith in God than to believe in nothing. But James classified this type of faith as equivalent to what demons believe:

Are there still some among you who hold that "only believing" is enough? Believing in one God? Well, remember that the demons believe this too – so strongly that they tremble in terror! (James 2:19)

If someone does not know Jesus, He is knocking at the door of their heart. We can encourage people to open the door!

IT MATTERS WHAT YOU SAY

Your words matter. It matters what you believe and it matters what you say.

If there is a person you love, does it matter what you say about them? Yes!

Does it matter what we say about Jesus? Should we clearly state what we believe about Him? When we are asked if we believe that He is our Savior, should we say, "I hope so" or, "Yes, I know He is"?

When we are asked if we are going to Heaven should we say, "I hope so"? If we say that, what does it mean? Does it mean that Jesus will take us to Heaven if He is able to do so? Or that He will take us to Heaven if we are good enough? If He only takes to Heaven those who are good enough, would He take anyone?

Think about what you would say, because it matters. It matters to the people to whom you have an opportunity to speak and to God.

MARY

A young girl was visited by an angel who told her:

The Holy Spirit shall come upon you, and the power of God shall overshadow you; so the baby born to you will be utterly holy – the Son of God. (Luke 1:35)

Mary's response to the angel was:

I am the Lord's servant, and I am willing to do whatever he wants. May everything you said come true. (Luke 1:38)

Mary was confronted with an "impossible" promise; and she

responded with unusual faith. She simply believed. As a result, she is the most highly honored woman who has ever lived.

Having faith to believe what God promises is often difficult. We want evidence. Throughout the Bible, God demonstrates His desire to bless anyone who will simply believe what He says.

Jesus came to tell us of God's unusual promise. God would give us Christ's righteousness as a free gift if we would believe His Son. Because we are humans we want evidence. We want to see clear evidence that we have Christ's righteousness. When we see clear evidence that we are not like Christ, we may decide to believe that God's promise is not fulfilled in us. We would lose the power to be the instrument in God's hands that Mary the mother of Jesus was!

Mary fulfilled her mission. You and I can fulfill our mission. We can tell others about God's desire to give us His free gift of eternal life. The more we believe His promise, the more effective we become! We will have the wonderful power of God's Holy Spirit to help us.

THE UNIVERSE

It takes faith to believe what we are told about our universe. Astronomers tell us things that are beyond our ability to comprehend. God designed our universe to show His incomprehensible glory:

The heavens are telling the glory of God; they are a marvelous display of his craftsmanship. (Psalms 19:1)

For example, the sun does not look as big as our earth, but it could actually hold one million of our earth. Many things are not what they seem. The size of our sun is like a grain of sand compared to the size of the universe!

Think of the sun as the size of a dot (such as above the letter "i"). Use that tiny dot to measure the size of our own galaxy. If such dots were made from the Atlantic to the Pacific Ocean, that would represent the size of just our galaxy! One of those dots represents the sun. And our galaxy represents a tiny dot compared to the universe! God's craftsmanship is beyond our imagination.

How big is the universe that God created? To simplify that question, astronomers measure its size in light years. How many seconds do you think it takes light to go around our earth? At 186,000 miles per second, the answer is seven times in one second! It takes a bit of faith to believe that. It would take 27,000 years for light to travel across our own tiny galaxy. That takes even more faith to believe!

Remember that our own galaxy is a tiny speck in our universe!

How big is our universe? No one knows! We know that there are billions, yes billions, of galaxies. Many of them are far larger than our own.

How long would it take light to travel from here to the end of the entire universe? Astronomers are now wise enough to say, "We don't know." It would take at least millions of years for light to go from here to there. And no one knows why the universe is still expanding! We smile and think, "God knows!"

God made it extremely easy for us to believe that He exists and that He has the power to give us the free gift of eternal life if we believe what He tells us. I believe Him and what I believe gives me ever-increasing joy!

TEMPTATION

Temptation is a weapon that Satan has used ever since it worked on Adam and Eve. The number of Satan's tactics is countless.

He causes a man to become angry. Anger can become a rage that results in murder. When you and I are angry we may be tempted to speak harsh words that hurt people and tempt them to respond with their own anger. Anger can result in broken homes and that has forever been one of Satan's goals.

You may be tempted by alcohol, eating too much, drugs, or many other self-destroying temptations. You may remember things you have done, and think, "Why did I do that? You were tempted.

Satan will stop at nothing to destroy us, but remember God has provided a way for us to defeat every harmful temptation! Every one! He proclaims to us:

But now you are free from the power of sin and are slaves of God, and his benefits to you include holiness and everlasting life. (Romans 6:22)

What a joy it is to be a child of the One who loves us so much that He gave His only Son to die, so that we could be free from the power of sin and Satan's temptations.

Am I mentioning Satan too much? Perhaps you have seldom heard his name. People seldom even swear in his name. In the Bible, "Satan," "the devil" and "evil spirits" are mentioned 112 times! The Bible tells us a lot about Satan and we need to be well aware of what he is doing. Jesus said Satan is the father of lies! Eloquent speakers can convince us that something is true but later we learn that they were deliberately lying. Satan is far more convincing.

We pray in Jesus' name because He has power over Satan. When we trust in Jesus we can be absolutely certain that He has the power to take care of us both in life and in eternity!

EVIL SPIRITS

If we believe that Jesus is who He says He is, we need to understand that even evil spirits believe that. Yet that does not prepare them for Heaven! When they saw Jesus they would:

Fall down before him shrieking, "You are the Son of God!" (Mark 3:11)

One day Jesus encountered a man who was possessed by many demons:

"Send us into those hogs," the demons begged. And Jesus gave them permission. Then the evil spirits came out of the man and entered the hogs, and the entire herd plunged

down the steep hillside into the lake and drowned. (Mark 5:12-13)

The evil spirits were forced to do exactly what Jesus told them. God treats you and me as His children. We are free to trust Him if that is what we choose to do! Believing that Jesus is our Savior prepares us for eternity with Him.

Satan is our adversary and he knows when we are afraid.

A dog that wants to chase a man can tell if he is afraid by the man's smell. Even if the man pretends to be unafraid the dog knows the truth. If a confident man advances, the dog will stop. But if a fearful man moves toward an angry dog, it will attack.

God knows that Satan will attack us when we are afraid. God wants to help us so He provided a way for us to be unafraid. When we know that God has written our names in Heaven we will be confident. If we only hope that we are His children we will be afraid that we are unworthy of His protection.

God tells us to:

Put on all of God's armor so that you will be able to stand safe against all strategies and tricks of Satan. (Ephesians 6:11)

This armor includes God's written promises. When we believe them, His promises defeat the fear that Satan tries to use against us. When we take up the sword of the Spirit and begin to understand the power that is available to us, Satan may say, "It's only natural for you to be afraid." Natural? Yes. But God wants us to have supernatural faith in His Son!

TAX COLLECTORS

Dishonest tax collectors and other notorious sinners often came to listen to Jesus' sermons. (Luke 15:1)

Why did this happen? Jesus welcomed sinners!

Who is a sinner? Who is not a sinner? Your answers to those questions are crucial to an understanding that God wants to give you the free gift of eternal life!

Satan repeatedly, over and over, year after year, tries to convince us that we are too sinful to be absolutely positive that we are going to Heaven. He gives us clear and specific evidence of our sin. If we listen to these accusations how can we dare approach a Holy God?

God opens His arms to anyone who comes to Him and confesses that they are a sinner who believes in Jesus as Savior. We dare not leave His presence and then say He did not promise to give us eternal life. Jesus died in order to give us eternal life as His gift to us.

But if we, by our testimony, declare that we do not have that free gift, we will be doing exactly what Satan wants us to do!

Yes, we are sinners, but that isn't all we are. We are forgiven sinners when we believe Jesus. I will never forget the joy that came into me when I believed that God had completely forgiven me. If He had told me, "Merlin, you must never disobey Me or I will take away this gift I have given you," I would soon have lost all my joy. But since I believed Him and believe Him still, He has continued to increase my faith and joy in His promise.

UNLIMITED OPPORTUNITIES

You are surrounded by unlimited opportunities to worry about this or that, and you have this or that reason to doubt that good things are true.

When you tell people that they can know with absolute assurance that they are going to Heaven, they may hear your words and think, "Maybe that's true for you, but not for me." That's why we need the confidence that God wants to give us.

God's promise to give anyone who believes Him the free gift of eternal life is the most wonderful promise and yet the most difficult for many people to believe. That's why we need to know what we believe and why. We have unlimited opportunities to share God's wonderful promise!

In the period of time after Jesus had ascended to Heaven God helped some men to believe His Good News. He permitted them to be placed in situations where they had an abundance of time to hear His message (like in prison cells). They carefully recorded His words. Now you and I can read and reread those words until they are chiseled into our thoughts. Then we can say with confidence, "God gives me His free gift of eternal life because Jesus died for me. He gave me His righteousness. I will be with Him forever!" People will hear His words through us.

POWER IN OUR FAITH

When they learn about God's free gift some folks have said, "If I can receive God's forgiveness so easily I might as well sin as much as I want and then ask for forgiveness."

There is one big problem with that idea. We can die before that same day is over. The Bible tells us that it is a fearsome thing to tempt God.

Besides all that, there is no sin that is as enjoyable as knowing we are children of God.

The strongest power that we have is our

faith in God. There is no security in anything else.

Today we could lose health, family, home, freedom, money, or anything else we value. But our faith assures us that nothing can be taken from or added to our lives unless God permits it.

By faith we can receive answers to our prayers, joy in our hearts, and confidence in God's protection. Without faith we could become victims of the many torments that Satan loves to use. Lest you think I mention his name too frequently, remember that he is mentioned 112 times in the Bible. God wants us to know that he is real.

People without faith try to put up a good front but inwardly they are afraid of death and the unknown. The stronger our own faith becomes the better we will be able to answer their questions. They have good reason to be afraid, but we can lead them to joy and peace in Jesus.

Those who wear eyeglasses do not have to clean them. They could go days or weeks without doing so. But gradually their ability to see would decline.

Our ability to grow in faith is the same. To prevent loss of faith we must draw close to God:

And when you draw close to God, God will draw close to you. Wash your hands, you sinners, and let your hearts be filled with

God alone to make them pure and true to him.
(James 4:8)

FOR SURE

Many medical tests prove that our bodies
are injured by our own feelings of distress.
God surely knows this; so He told us not to
be troubled about anything. He knew that
we would be tempted to worry about what
would happen to us when we die. When we
are young and healthy we may not think
about this. But when sickness, age or danger
threaten, we do think about life after death,
whether we want to or not. I have seen this
happen so many times during combat that
I know for sure what happens to men who
have not believed in God or life after death.

The dark cloud of approaching death
gets men's attention regardless of what they
believe. While I was an Army chaplain I often
talked with men about this. Some unbelievers
were convinced that I knew what I was talking
about. I believe that was one of the reasons
God had me there. I am now convinced that
He wants me to tell many unbelievers that
there is life after death and we can know,
for sure, what will happen to us. Our Father
tells us:

Trust God from the bottom of your heart;

don't try to figure out everything on your own.
(Proverbs 3:5 MSG)

JESUS' PROMISE

Jesus repeatedly promised to forgive our sins and give us His free gift of eternal life. Do you think that Jesus would not keep His promise?

Why did Jesus and His disciples speak so often about the free gift that God was offering? If something is "free" there is nothing that anyone can do to earn it. Yet our enemy, Satan, will tell us over and over that we have not yet done what we need to do to deserve Heaven.

The fleshly part of our nature *wants to deserve* the gift of eternal life and to spend our life trying to do better. The Holy Spirit is telling us that God wants us to *love and trust Him*. Doing those two things is sufficient to keep us happily busy for every minute of our lives.

Learning to love God more will cause us to seek His approval for everything we do or even think. Learning to love others more will cause us to seek ways to lead them to God's Son. God selected His plan of salvation so that more people would want people to know and love Him.

Some folks are tempted to think, "God must have an ego problem." No, God designed His plan for poor sinners like you and me. From the time we were in our mother's arms we have wanted to be loved. When we realize how much God loves us, one of our deepest, inborn needs, is satisfied!

HAPPINESS HERE ON EARTH

I'm the happiest person I know. Can I prove this to you? No, it is not something I can prove. Anyhow, that is not what I want to do. I want to help you be the happiest person that you know. Why? That is one of the very best ways for us to fall in love with God.

Jesus tried to help us have peace of mind through our faith in Him. He kept demonstrating what He could accomplish, but many people were unable to believe Him.

Jesus' disciples saw Him change water into wine, walk on water, bring fish into their nets, feed thousands of people, heal the sick, and even raise the dead, but they still did not have the faith in Him that He wanted them to have. Why not? They were humans just like you and me. When storms raged they were worried. When they wanted to walk on water they were afraid. When threatened with bodily harm they deserted Him. Later they received His Good News and learned to believe Him. That is how we can experience lasting happiness here on earth.

Satan is always trying to convince us that he can give us happy lives. But we know that he gives us the exact opposite. He is experienced at doing this without our realizing it. He will say, "John Doe is plotting a way to hurt you." If we believe him we begin to fret about what John may do. John is probably too busy with his own troubles to be even thinking about us. And why is he troubled? Because Satan has whispered something to him.

Happiness is only found in God. Do you want to be happy? Have faith in Him! When you lack faith, study what the Bible says about Him and eventually you will confirm what Jesus said:

Seek and you will find. Knock, and the door will be opened. (Matthew 7:7)

OUR SOURCE OF HAPPINESS

Jesus said:

Anything is possible if you have faith. (Mark 9:23)

Have faith? Faith in what? Faith that God will make us happy? No. Jesus is telling us to have faith in God. Happiness is a result of our believing Him:

Don't worry about anything; instead, pray about everything; tell God your needs and don't forget to thank him for his answers. If you do this you will experience God's peace, which is far more wonderful than the human mind can understand. His peace will keep your thoughts and your hearts quiet and at rest as you trust in Christ Jesus. (Philippians 4:6-7)

Don't worry about anything? But there are so many things to worry about! Yes, and these things are brought to our minds by Satan. He wants everyone to be as unhappy as he is. He can take anything and cause us to worry about it just as he did with Adam and Eve!

Jesus repeatedly urged His disciples not to be worried or anxious about anything. They worried about things that could not possibly happen! Jesus had told them what they would do after He was resurrected. Their destiny was fixed! What Jesus promised happened. They became mighty warriors in building the church, just as Jesus said they would.

You and I can be victorious over everything, just as Jesus promised. But our faith must be based on what He tells us. We can study His words and know what He says.

MIRACLES

Anyone whose Father is God listens gladly to the words of God. Since you don't, it proves you aren't his children. (John 8:47)

Jesus was speaking to the religious leaders of His day. Their spiritual ears were deaf.

Jesus spoke to dead people and told them to come back to life. He speaks to us through His Word!

Without His miracle working power we could not bring our spiritually dead bodies back to life. When we believe in and trust in Him as our Savior, He says, "Come to life," and our names are recorded in Heaven! How glad I am that Satan has no access to that book!

Long ago, even before he made the world, God chose us to be his very own, through what Christ would do for us; he decided then to make us holy in his eyes, without a single fault – we who stand before him covered with his love. His unchanging plan has always been to adopt us into his own family by sending Jesus Christ to die for us. And he did this because he wanted to! . . .

So overflowing is his kindness toward us that he took away all our sins through the blood of his Son, by whom we are saved. (Ephesians 1:4-5, 7)

When we hear the words "Have faith in

God" we may cringe because we feel that we are unable to work miracles.

Dozens of times every day we can increase our faith by using it to accomplish small things. When tempted to be irritated we can believe that God will use that irritation to work good in us. At times this may seem to be impossible to do, but Jesus said we could do anything by faith. After we receive the faith not to be irritated with one small annoyance, our faith takes one step forward. Every time we exercise our faith in God our faith will grow, whether we feel it or not! Eventually we can smile and rejoice that God is keeping His promise:

Ask, and you will be given what you ask for. (Matthew 7:7)

Ask and keep on asking.

The reverse is also true. If we continue giving in to negative thoughts and feelings, they keep growing. Eventually they seem to be so much a part of us that we keep doing the same thing over and over. We become ill-tempered people!

IN THE ARMY NOW

In the Army I was trained to look for the enemy and then look some more. They could be hiding in front of us and we would not see them until it was too late. One sharpshooter could end my life.

I was also trained as a sharpshooter. We learned to hide so we wouldn't be seen. We could hit an enemy and his comrades would have difficulty knowing where we were.

Satan has been learning all the tricks of a sharpshooter for thousands of years. He does not want to be seen! We must learn how to detect where he is.

In our training, sharpshooters would hide in front of us and then suddenly reveal themselves so we could see that in combat we would be dead because we had been careless. We must learn and be aware of Satan's tactics.

There is no need to be paranoid but we need to look and then look some more! As we read and study Jesus' words we learn ways to know our enemy's strategies.

ENJOYING ARGUING

Some people enjoy arguing about Christianity and the Bible. They insist that they do not believe that faith in Jesus is the only way to Heaven. They say there are many religions that also claim to be the one true faith. I ask them what they know about Jesus and what He taught. Their usual response is that they have not studied the Bible. They have made little to no effort to know for themselves if

Jesus is who He said He was.

If a man tells me that he was a General Officer in the U.S. Army I would know what questions to ask him to help me know if he is telling the truth.

If you should tell me that you have done your best to have faith in Jesus, I would ask you what words of His you remember. If you know almost nothing about what Jesus taught I would know that you had not made a sincere effort to have faith in Him.

Each of us will make an honest effort to know and understand whatever we want to understand. Jesus said to some who did not believe in Him as Savior that they weren't listening to God:

But you are not listening to him, for you refuse to believe me – the one sent to you with God's message. (John 5:38)

Take Jesus' words seriously! If we want to know about Him we must know what He said. Feel the emphasis in His words:

I say emphatically that anyone who listens to my message and believes in God who sent me has eternal life, and will never be damned for his sins, but has already passed out of death into life. (John 5:24)

What a promise: we have already passed out of death into life!

THE STING OF DEATH

Of this we are sure: we are going to die. We do not know when or how. That may cause us to worry, until we know the secret of looking forward to Heaven:

O death, where then your victory? Where then your sting? (1 Corinthians 15:55)

Because of Jesus we need not fear death! The sting of death is the fear it creates. We realize that we have broken God's laws and could not survive a simple test on just the Ten Commandments.

I have lived with many men who feared death. It lurked behind every hill, every bend in the road, every tree, everywhere!

Preparing to jump out of an airplane often causes men to become completely paralyzed. They are humiliated later when they realize what has happened. They do not intend to be afraid nor do they want to be paralyzed with fear. But fear does not ask for our permission.

Death doesn't ask for our permission either. We may pray, plead and beg for more time to better prepare for death, but 100% of us will die.

Jesus offered us forgiveness for every weakness, failure and sin. For most of us that would be a lot of forgiveness. But if we try to make peace with God by living a good life, death has the painful sting of fear. Why try to make our own way when Jesus promised to take the penalty of our sins if we place our trust in Him? I prefer to put my trust in Jesus and I invite you to do the same.

THE JUDGMENT SEAT

Paul wrote:

Remember, each of us will stand personally before the Judgment Seat of God. (Romans 14:10)

That thought could make us tremble, but we rejoice in the knowledge that we are given Jesus' righteousness when we believe in Him!

So there is now no condemnation awaiting those who belong to Christ Jesus. (Romans 8:1)

I spoke with a person who seemed to have faith in Jesus as Savior. When I asked them, "Do you believe you were forgiven of all your sins when you believed in Jesus as Savior?" they immediately said, "Yes," with great assurance. So I asked another question.

"Whenever you sin do you ask God to forgive you?"

"Yes, I try to always do that."

"If you forget to do so, what do you do then?"

"I pray regularly that He will forgive all my sins."

"But what would happen to you if you sin and are in an accident and are killed before you have asked for forgiveness?"

The person had a very unhappy look.

"I don't know," came the reply, "and that thought scares me."

I then explained that because of our faith in Jesus, God judges us as His child. His knows exactly what is in our heart. If we have a heart that wants to please Him, but sometimes fails, He knows that. What we do is not the basis of our forgiveness. We are forgiven because of what Jesus has done.

BOOK OF GALATIANS

I recommend that you read the book of Galatians. Frequently. It has only six chapters and records Paul's passionate plea for all Christians to cling to God's Good News.

About 22 years after Jesus' death, Paul recognized that Christians were already beginning to believe that they could earn their salvation by good works. He realized that men were teaching a false doctrine and ignoring Christ's message. You can feel the passion in his heart as he wrote:

I am not one of those who treats Christ's death as meaningless. For if we could be saved by keeping Jewish laws, then there was no need for Christ to die. (Galatians 2:21)

Shortly after Jesus ascended into Heaven some began to lose faith in His message. They believed there was danger in the simple message of salvation by faith. They decided that people would be lured into sin if they thought they had eternal life as a free gift from God. But the opposite was happening. People lost the power, joy and assurance of salvation by faith, and they lost the joy of telling others about Jesus! The church was emphasizing what people needed to do rather than what Jesus had done for them.

Paul raised his voice with increasing fervor:

Oh, foolish Galatians! What magician has hypnotized you and cast an evil spell upon you? For you used to see the meaning of Jesus Christ's death as clearly as though I had waved a placard before you with a picture on it of Christ dying on the cross. (Galatians 3:1)

Jesus knew that men would soon distort God's Good News, so after His ascension into Heaven He came back to teach Paul the essentials of salvation by faith. Paul did his best to tell everyone.

Paul wrote to those who were losing their trust in Christ for salvation:

Have you gone completely crazy? For if trying to obey the Jewish laws never gave you spiritual life in the first place, why do you think that trying to obey them now will make you stronger Christians? (Galatians 3:3)

Paul goes on to remind them:

You have suffered so much for the Gospel. Now are you going to just throw it all overboard? I can hardly believe it! (Galatians 3:4)

Yes, hardly believable, but many religious people do not know that what Paul was so concerned about was replacing salvation by faith with keeping God's laws. Paul tells the Galatians that they must stop thinking about obeying laws and turn back to believing and trusting in Christ.

Galatians 3:11 tells us:

God has said that the only way we can be right in His sight is by faith.

We rejoice with Paul as he teaches us how different it is to be saved by faith rather than by the Law, which tells us that we must obey every law without one slip. Who could do that? No one.

Some men ask why God gave the law if He knew we could not keep it. Paul clearly explains that God gave the law so we could see how guilty we are of displeasing Him and see our need for His Good News:

The only way out is through faith in Jesus Christ; the way of escape is open to all who believe him. (Galatians 3:22)

GROWING IN FAITH

Be careful – watch out for attacks from Satan, your great enemy. He prowls around like a hungry, roaring lion, looking for some victim to tear apart. (1 Peter 5:8)

Satan wants to tear us apart.

You have a weakness; I know you do. We all do. I don't like mine and you probably do not like yours. The question is, how do we deal with our flaws? It took me years to realize that by faith in God's promises I could deal with my failures.

Shall I tell you one of mine? Maybe it will help you deal with your own.

Whatever I do, when I am finished I have a dreadful feeling that I failed. It may be the Devil's way of tormenting me or it may be God's way of keeping me humble.

I have preached thousands of sermons to some small and some very large audiences. While preaching I always feel joy and am singing in my heart over the opportunity God has given me. But at the conclusion I always feel that I could have done much better.

I also have the feeling that I could have done much better after I've talked to a person about Jesus.

Why am I telling you this? Because I know that Satan has decided what his best tactic is for tempting each one of us. He even tried his method on Jesus. Jesus resisted! You and I can also be victorious.

My method is to follow God's guidelines. He tells us to always be thankful, so when a defeated thought comes to my mind I rejoice that God is working for my good. He doesn't want me to be proud so He permits Satan to tell me how poorly I have done. Usually I have to thank God over and over until His peace, once again, takes control of my mind.

Have faith that God will work your problem out for your good, and your faith will grow!

GARDEN OF EDEN

But I am frightened, fearing that in some way you will be led away from your pure and simple devotion to our Lord, just as Eve was deceived by Satan in the Garden of Eden. (2 Corinthians 11:3)

Before the fall, Adam and Eve had never sinned. God told them there was only one thing they should not do. They disobeyed Him.

Paul warned that Satan could also convince us to believe what is not true. He said we could be convinced not to believe the simple message that Jesus gave us: believe in Him as Savior, and God gives you eternal life. Too simple? That's what Satan has convinced many people to believe.

Satan asked Eve what God had said they could not eat. Eve said God had told them there was one fruit they could not eat or touch, or they would die.

Satan told Eve they would not die if they ate the forbidden fruit, but that they would become as wise as God if they did eat it.

Eve looked at the forbidden fruit and saw that it looked good to eat, was pleasant to the eyes, and was very desirable. She decided it would make them as wise as God, just as Satan had told her. She ate the fruit and then gave some to Adam.

As Satan had said, their eyes were opened. They saw that they were naked. Now they needed clothes so they used fig tree leaves to cover themselves.

God came to talk with them, as He had previously done, and asked Adam why he was hiding. Adam said Eve had given him the forbidden fruit and he had eaten it. God asked Eve why she had done this and she said it was Satan's fault.

Satan has not given up! He still tells us to look and see for ourselves. Forbidden things look good and desirable. He says we will enjoy them and will see for ourselves what they can do for us. But like Adam and Eve we are then forced to live without the good things that God wants to give us.

By faith in Jesus we can receive the good things that God wants to give us, like joy and peace now, and eternal life in Heaven.

Satan says, "You must first learn how to live holy lives before you will know that you are going to Heaven." But Jesus said we are saved only by our faith in Him.

Remember the lesson from the Garden of Eden!

GOD LOVES US!

The Lord our God is the one and only God. And you must love him with all your heart and soul and mind and strength. (Mark 12:29-30)

Jesus said this is our most important goal. Our goal is to love God. How much does God love us? The Bible is clear on that point:

God loved the world so much that he gave his only Son so that anyone who believes in him shall not perish but have eternal life. (John 3:16)

Without realizing why, I once was afraid of God. The most important thing I have learned is that God loves me far more than I have ever loved Him. He is love!

God is love. (1 John 4:8)

Learning how much God loves me has changed my relationship with Him. I do not fear His judgment because I know He has already taken care of that and has received me as one of His adopted sons. He knows my mistakes but He also knows that I want to please Him.

God doesn't love us because we are good people. His Son has given us His righteousness. When Satan attacks me I often think of God's loving protection.

Consider the good things that come to us when we believe in someone or something. One of my great blessings is my certainty that my wife, Mary, loves me. When I see that our children love me I am thankful to them and to God. When friends show me that they love me they bring me joy. Being loved is a great joy. God asks us to love Him.

But if a person isn't loving and kind, it shows that he doesn't know God – for God is love. (1 John 4:8)

Jesus is now preparing a place for each of us in Heaven. Why? Because He loves us! It will be far better than anything I could ever deserve. I can visualize a sign on the front door: Merlin lives here. Under that a signature: Jesus. He said:

There are many homes up there where my Father lives, and I am going to prepare them for your coming. When everything is ready, then I will come and get you, so that you can always be with me where I am. If this weren't so, I would tell you plainly. (John 14:2-3)

MY PREPARATION

Each of us has different characteristics. We enjoy doing some things but not others. I recently realized how different I am from many men. Why did God make me this way?

Some men like physical activities. Others like artistic work such as painting and music. I like both. I think that God wanted to prepare me to be receptive to whatever He wanted to teach me. I'll list some of my interests and perhaps that will help you to better understand the person I am.

When I was eleven-years-old my father bought me a large bag of firecrackers. After telling me to be careful, he permitted me to set them off as I pleased. After enjoying some of them I wondered what it would be like to make a large explosion. I took a broomstick, wrapped a section with newspaper, tied it with string and then removed the paper from the broomstick. Next I folded in the bottom of the paper so it would hold powder. I poured the powder from about thirty firecrackers into my new creation. Then I attached a wick to the top so I could make my "big explosion."

It worked. Everyone around our home heard it. I was elated at my invention.

All my life I have enjoyed finding new things to learn. In grade school only "sissies" played marbles but I decided to learn. We played for "keeps" and I usually walked away with a pocket full of shinny treasures. At the same time I thoroughly enjoyed playing football. In college and in the Army I enjoyed being on both the football and the baseball teams.

I learned to love playing checkers (never been beaten), chess and, unfortunately, poker.

In the Army I volunteered to become a paratrooper, demolition expert, jungle expert and sharpshooter.

I worked to become a commissioned pilot with CAP (Civil Air Patrol). I loved flying my own planes, ice-skating, snorkeling, water and snow skiing, and boating on motorboats or sailboats. I loved ping-pong, badminton, horseshoes, bowling, flying large kites, and learning to make apple cider.

I enjoyed hunting rabbits, squirrels, pheasants, deer and bears (I have a picture of a bear that nearly ate me), as well as fishing for trout or salmon, training and riding horses, and training dogs.

During this same time I was also involved in drawing pictures, painting with oils (the paintings hang on our living room walls), playing the saxophone, piano, guitar and a mouth organ at the same time.

God designed me to enjoy all of these things, but best of all He is teaching me to know and love Him. The very best thing He has given me is a longing to love Him more. No one will have a happy heart until they know His love. He was willing to come to earth and be hated and humiliated by men in order to give us His free gift of eternal life.

BREAKING BAD HABITS

Bad habits are difficult to break, but not impossible if we know how.

Using our own will power is usually difficult. With some habits every cell in our body can work against us. Our minds say, "Just enjoy yourself."

So what alternative do we have? Jesus told us to ask and believe. In yourself? No! Believe that God will help. He created us and He can control every cell in our body.

Our only problem is learning to believe. You can begin by saying, "God, I believe You deliver me from this habit." Every time you think of it, say it again, "Lord, I believe You deliver me." Say it 10, 100 or 1,000 times a day. If your faith fails, say, "God, I believe you forgive me. And I believe You are helping me."

Your enemy hates to hear such talk. But God wants to hear you declare your faith in Him. He will help you to be victorious:

Ask, and you will be given what you ask

for. Seek, and you will find. Knock, and the door will be opened. (Matthew 7:7)

You and I may ask and then doubt that we receive. But we can gradually learn to believe for one thing, and then believe for another. How long does it take for us to learn? It depends on how long we have been practicing not believing.

If you have never had a direct answer to your prayers, think of how excited you will be!

REMEMBERING

You may remember eating a sandwich while concentrating on a good television program. Later you remember eating but very little about how it tasted. We remember whatever we concentrate on.

We can read the Bible without concentrating on what it says. You may have memorized John 3:16 and still be able to repeat it, but have almost no understanding of what the verse means.

God so loved the world. What do those words mean to you? That the Creator of the universe actually loved you so much that He permitted men to torture and crucify His only Son for you? Do you believe that really happened? Do you think that if you believe in His Son, God will give you eternal life?

What did God mean when He used the word "believe"? That Jesus lived here on earth? Not hardly. Some men saw Him and knew He was here but still did not believe in Him. Or believe that He was crucified? No, that cannot be what God requires because men watched Jesus be crucified and still did not believe that He was God's Son.

Jesus told us the story of a rich man who died and went to Hell where he was tormented. He looked into Heaven and saw a beggar named Lazarus sitting with Abraham. The rich man begged to have the former beggar come to him, dip his finger in water and cool his tongue. That request was denied. So he asked if he might go back to see his five brothers and warn them about the suffering in Hell.

Abraham told the rich man that his brothers could learn all they needed to know if they would listen to Moses and the prophets. If they did not listen to the Word of God, Abraham said, they would not listen to a man who came back from the dead to warn them.

God requires us to believe what His Son said. Do you remember what His Son said? Jesus asked us to believe that He came to give us the free gift of eternal life. Have you ever concentrated on those words? Do you believe that He has given you that gift? Jesus' words are available to us. If we do not read them we will eventually stand before God and have no excuse for what we did not read!

BEING CONFIDENT

I am not confident that I will be alive tomorrow. I'm not ill and feel I could live for years. But that's no guarantee.

I am confident, however, that if I die tomorrow I will go to be with Jesus. I am absolutely sure.

All my trust and hope rest in my faith in what Jesus taught us. Faith in Him causes me to rejoice in today, tomorrow, and in all eternity.

This faith is so clear to me that I would not exchange it for anything. A skeptic may say, "Merlin, you are just believing what you want to believe." Yes, this is what I want to believe, but the reason I believe it is because Jesus said it. It has proved to be the very best for me.

I've come very close to death several times and every time I felt the joy of knowing where I was going. I have been with many people who thought they might soon die and they were frightened and unhappy. They helped convince me that what I believe is not only what I want to believe, but what Jesus wants me to believe.

If you are unsure about whether or not you are going to heaven, I hope and pray that you carefully study this book. You can be confident!

SPREAD THE WORD

Abraham received righteousness because He did one thing that pleased God. He believed Him:

For the Scriptures tell us Abraham believed God, and that is why God canceled his sins and declared him "not guilty." (Romans 4:3)

Most people are quite willing to admit that they are sinners but are afraid of declaring that they have received the righteousness of Christ. Without realizing it they are refusing to do what God tells us to do:

And now, through Christ, all the kindness of God has been poured out upon us undeserving sinners; and now he is sending us out around the world to tell all people everywhere the great things God has done for them, so that they, too, will believe and obey him. (Romans 1:5)

We are commissioned to spread the Word! How foolish it would be to refuse to obey this command because we somehow believe it does not apply to us. How foolish we would be if we did not believe in God's decision to lavish His kindness upon us undeserving sinners:

Now God says he will accept and acquit us – declare us "not guilty" – if we trust Jesus Christ to take away our sins. And we all can be saved in this same way, by coming to Christ, no matter who we are or what we have been like. (Romans 3:22)

When the enormity of what Jesus has done for us dawns on us, we begin to enjoy the peace that He had. He believed that God loved Him and that He would soon go to be with Him. When we know that we will soon be with Him we want to spread the Word about the free gift we have received. We do not know how He will use us but we believe that He will. We even enjoy expecting what God is going to do in and through us! Gradually we know that we can somehow become more like Jesus.

The Jews tried so hard to be what God wanted them to be but they neglected the one thing He wanted: faith in what He could do for them! God gave us His simple formula:

If you tell others with your own mouth that Jesus Christ is your Lord, and believe in your own heart that God has raised him from the dead, you will be saved. For it is by believing in his heart that a man becomes right with God; and with his mouth he tells others of his faith, confirming his salvation. (Romans 10:9-10)

BE HONEST

Be honest with God!

He knows what you are thinking and what you believe.

The father of a boy who had an evil spirit brought his son to Jesus. Jesus told the father to have faith in Him. The father replied:

I do have faith; oh, help me to have more! (Mark 9:24)

Jesus healed the son and showed us that we need to cry out to God when we are in earnest about wanting His help.

If you want to believe that Jesus is able to give you eternal life, tell God. Then ask Him to help you believe.

Talk with believers. Do everything you would do to find the answer to any other important question. Study the Bible:

And so it is with prayer – keep on asking and you will keep on getting; keep on looking and you will keep on finding; knock and the door will be opened. (Luke 11:9)

We dare not be lazy when we seek God's help. He wants our honest, earnest efforts to know and do His will. God wants us to first do our best when we want to receive His help.

How long will this take? Maybe one second. He doesn't care what you have done; He cares about what is in your heart.

You will forever be glad that you were honest with God!

Faith in Jesus is not half-hearted. God requires a faith that He knows is real.

We have Jesus' promise:

When the Holy Spirit, who is truth, comes, he shall guide you into all truth. (John 16:13)

JESUS IN THE GARDEN

In the Garden of Gethsemane Jesus prayed:

If it is possible, let this cup be taken away from me. But I want your will, not mine. (Matthew 26:39).

He knew God would understand His heart, but first and foremost Jesus wanted God's will.

There will be times of suffering that we would like to avoid, but if we believe that God will work good for us, then we can face whatever comes!

You were very weak when you were first born but you grew in strength. We may be weak in faith and understanding when we are born again, but we can grow and keep on growing.

SHOUT UNTO GOD

O clap your hands, all ye people; shout unto God with the voice of triumph. (Psalms 47:1 KJV)

You may not like the idea of shouting or hand clapping. But this Scripture should not be ignored – for your own benefit.

Why should we shout to God? He wants us to believe that we are triumphant.

People shouted to Jesus because they believed He could help them. It wasn't their shouts that caused Him to help them, but their faith. The Bible often says that Jesus saw people's faith.

Revelation 3:19 (KJV) says:

Be zealous therefore, and repent.

God wants us to approach Him zealously and then to be zealous in what we do for Him.

As a paratrooper I was taught to be zealous when I jumped out of an airplane. Initially this was not easy to understand! But we needed to look up and leap out of the airplane, not fall out. Sounds strange, I know, but it was necessary.

If we simply fell out we would look down and our heads would quickly be drawn lower than our feet. If that happened, several bad things could follow: Our parachute could catch on the airplane's tail! That would not be good. Or we could become so entangled with the parachute that the lines would wrap around us! Also, not good.

So we were taught to stand in the door, look up, and quickly leap upward. If we hesitated we could force our buddies to jump late and miss the "drop zone." In practice and in combat that could cause men to lose their lives. Again, not good.

Learning to jump out of an airplane taught me much about the damage fear can do. Whenever I feel its tentacles reaching into my heart I plead with God to cause His Holy Spirit to fill my heart with faith.

Leave the plane quickly and correctly.

God says look up, jump and be enthusiastic.

We need to understand that our zeal impacts the eternal life of others. We may have only one opportunity to show or tell someone what they need to hear about Jesus! If we hesitate, they may suffer.

FEELING DESERTED

Jesus was beaten so cruelly that His features no longer resembled those of a human being. His hands and feet were nailed to a cross. What malicious torture Satan arranged in this, his final opportunity to defeat Jesus. During this final battle against evil, as Jesus bore the sins of the world, He cried out to His Father:

My God, my God, why have you deserted me? (Mark 15:34)

You and I may feel the same way when the same enemy attacks us. Satan often waits until we are weakened by sickness and pain. We need to prepare by growing in faith that God is our God. He is our Father. We are His children.

The older we get the more we realize that age brings problems we have never experienced before. We need to grow in spiritual strength – now – so we will be prepared for whatever temptations are thrust upon us.

I am greatly encouraged when I meditate on the fact that the only thing keeping me out of Heaven is life on earth! When this body is no more, then I will graduate. We need not fear death. We can rejoice in the joys that lie ahead because we know that we are God's children and He will never desert us!

While still on earth we can find new ways to rejoice now, and in the hereafter. When I recover from feeling ill, I nearly always think of how illness has helped me appreciate how good I feel when I am well.

In Heaven we may be able think back about the bad times we had on earth from the vantage point of the perfect home that God prepared for us!

DON'T WAIT FOR GOD – PART I

Don't wait for God to make you do something. Do what you can do.

When you feel like crying, try to sing. When you can't sing, hum. When you can't run, walk. When you can't walk, lean forward. When you can't stand, look up and expect God to do something.

I know these things from experience. God kept me doing what I could when there was nothing else I could do.

In college other students were selected to go to churches to speak. I wanted to do that, but instead I was offered the opportunity to clean the college restrooms.

The teachers all seemed to like me and appreciate my zeal, but they selected those who could speak well to do the preaching.

No one wanted to go to the local jail and hold services so I volunteered for that and had a wonderful time holding the cell bars, pleading with men to accept Jesus.

I do not remember ever feeling neglected or unwanted. I just kept looking for opportunities. Once I thought of holding a meeting in the center of the local town. I stood on the courthouse steps and gave my testimony over a public address system I had rented. People stopped to listen! I well remember how excited I was.

Years later I was invited to speak to an audience of 5,000.

My point is, God watches us. He sees what we do and knows why we do it. In His own time He opened new opportunities for a boy who did what he could, whenever and wherever he could. Years later I was invited to speak to an audience of 500,000! In our Escondido, California office there is a picture of that event.

Remember the shepherd boy, David? No one asked him to attack the giant. David saw what needed to be done and simply did it.

DON'T WAIT FOR GOD – PART II

Throughout the Bible men and women saw opportunities and did whatever needed to be done. And so when I began learning about the joy and power there is in praising the Lord I began to write a book, something I never thought I could do. I wrote and wrote, page after page.

Pastors began inviting me to speak in their churches. At first only small audiences, but then larger and larger audiences started to attend. I began to receive more and more invitations – come to our state, to our country. We will pay your way if you will come. Why? The only reason I can give is that God wanted doors to open for me to do what He wanted me to do. He took my lack of ability and poured zeal into my heart.

What will God do through you? That doesn't matter. Your job is to begin where you are, doing what you can do. Expect that God will do with you what He does with anyone who does what they can do.

Laugh, run, jump, sing, and always be thankful to God. He has a place reserved for you in Heaven where He can bless you for all eternity.

But first of all know that you believe in Jesus as your Savior and that He has written your name in God's Book of Eternal Life!

I'm sure you want to hear God say to you:

Well done, thou good and faithful servant: thou hast been faithful over a few things, I will make thee ruler over many things: enter thou into the joy of thy Lord. (Matthew 25:21 KJV)

DO IT LATER

When we have a task to accomplish we often think, "I'll do it later." What we put off now may be more difficult to do later.

Whether we put it off for an hour, a day or a month, it will always be waiting in the back of our minds. "I need to get that done." We begin to feel guilty and that influences our peace of mind.

We can learn to do things ASAP (as soon as possible). That may take time since we have so often said "I don't want to do it now."

Once the spirit of procrastination becomes embedded in us it severely decreases our ability to serve God. For example, the Holy Spirit may say to us, "Go to that person and tell them that God loves them," or "Give them a scripture verse," or something similar to encourage them to become a Christian. We respond, "Yes, I'll do that later." Then later becomes never.

I remember the man I felt impressed to ask to receive Jesus as Savior, and I did so. He did not accept Jesus. Within an hour he died in a car accident. I have been free of any guilty feelings, because I know I did my best. When I'm tempted to put off helping someone I often remember that man.

Please do your best to do what needs to be done as soon as you are able to do so. Your peace of mind will increase day by day.

MOCKINGBIRD'S SONG

While out walking, I heard a mocking bird singing its remarkable chorus of different melodies. I thought to myself, "I'm enjoying this beautiful music but he is not singing to please me. It's what God created him to do."

God created me to sing happy songs too, but He also gave me free will to do what I want to do. I can go through life grumbling about everything or I can learn to sing a happy song. So I sing while I'm out walking. While doing this I often learn new things. One is that as an old man I can still learn new, happy things!

I had forgotten how we used to march when I was a soldier. We held our heads high with our chin tucked in. I heard a whisper, "Hold your head high and tuck your chin in." I did and something happened. My entire body stood tall! My abdomen came in and stayed there as long as I kept my head held high. Remarkable!

As a senior I had learned to amble along with my abdomen sagging. Not good! I walked and felt like an old man. Now I often remember and practice my new plan of walking tall. It makes me feel younger and happier. Try it. Then try singing a happy song. You'll like it.

GOD'S LESSON PLAN

God explained His amazing plan to Ezekiel:
And I will give you a new heart – I will give you new and right desires – and put a new spirit within you. I will take out your stony

hearts of sin and give you new hearts of love.
(Ezekiel 36:26 KJV)

God wants to give us a new spirit and a new heart. Then we are ready to learn how to please Him. We can believe that we are His children. **We can learn with a happy heart!**

WHAT YOU BELIEVE

What you believe determines the amount of passion you have. That's true for anything. Our actions are guided by what we believe.

If you smell smoke in your home you check to see what is causing it. You may not have an urgent compulsion to run and check everything, but you do want to see what the problem is. You are not overly anxious because there may be a fire or there may not be.

If you see a fire it grabs all your attention! You immediately do something, and quickly! You know there is fire.

You do not think, "There is nothing I can do," or, "Maybe someone else will take care of it."

The fire creates a passion to do something, to take action!

What we believe about the things Jesus taught us determines how much passion we have to take action. He told us how we could help others to know Him and have eternal life. But if we are not zealous to get His message to them, they'll never know.

Jesus taught about a man who was in Hell and pleaded with God to let him go back to warn his brothers so they wouldn't make the same mistakes he had made. He was passionate about doing something! But God told him it was too late for him to help anyone.

The day will come when we will no longer be able to help anyone know about Jesus and what He taught us.

If our faith in what Jesus can do is feeble we will have only a slight desire to tell people about Him.

What you believe determines what you will do!

HAPPIER EVERY DAY

Yes, happier every day. Older and becoming happier? How could that be? My ancient physical body complains, but I've learned to hear a better voice. I read and reread the words in the Bible and they cause me to hear Jesus' voice more clearly. He is cheering me on and promising me a wonderful new body when I come home. Soon my eyes will open and there I will be – forever!

THIS BOOK HAS HELPED ME

Writing this book has strengthened my faith and it has greatly increased my love for God.

I pray it will help everyone who studies it.

Work hard so God can say to you, "Well done." Be a good workman, one who does not need to be ashamed when God examines your work. (2 Timothy 2:15)

The Bible has hundreds of verses that tell us exactly how we can know we are going to Heaven. If we want God to approve of us we need to know what He says!

I have put aside all else, counting it worth less than nothing, in order that I can have Christ, and become one with him, no longer counting on being saved by being good enough or by obeying God's laws, but by trusting Christ to save me; for God's way of making us right with himself depends on faith – counting on Christ alone. (Philippians 3:8)

For God in his wisdom saw to it that the world would never find God through human brilliance, and then he stepped in and saved all those who believed his message, which the world calls foolish and silly. (1 Corinthians 1:21)

For it is from God alone that you have your life through Christ Jesus. He showed us God's plan of salvation; he was the one who made us acceptable to God; he made us pure and holy and gave himself to purchase our salvation. (1 Corinthians 1:30)

Christ has brought you into the very presence of God, and you are standing there before him with nothing left against you – nothing left that he could even chide you for; The only condition is that you fully believe the Truth, standing in it steadfast and firm, strong in the Lord, convinced of the Good News that Jesus died for you, and never shifting from trusting him to save you. This is the wonderful news that came to each of you and is now spreading all over the world. And I, Paul, have the joy of telling it to others. (Colossians 1:22-23)

You and I can: **have the joy of telling it to others**.

If this book has been a blessing to you, please let us know. Each month we prepare *Praise News* in which we share new things that we have learned about praise. We will be pleased to send this to you at no charge if you request it.

Write to:
Merlin R. Carothers
PO Box 2518
Escondido, CA 92033-2518
www.foundationofpraise.org

Prison to Praise.. **$5**
Many say this is the most unusual book they have ever read and it changed their lives. This is not a book about a prison with bars, but about a prison of circumstances and how to be set free!

Prison to Praise, DVD..................................... **$10**

Power in Praise **$9**
Learn how the principles introduced in *Prison to Praise* work in every day life.

Answers to Praise **$9**
Overjoyed Christians felt compelled to share with Merlin the "signs and wonders" they experienced while practicing the teachings in his first two books.

Praise Works! **$9**
More letters from an assortment of thousands illustrate the secret of freedom through praise.

Walking and Leaping **$9**
When Merlin and his family rolled over a hill in their new car and trailer they praised the Lord and miracles happened!

Bringing Heaven into Hell................................. **$9**
Merlin shares new discoveries of how the Holy Spirit sheds light from heaven in the midst of a personal hell.

Victory on Praise Mountain **$9**
Spontaneous praise often leads into valleys that are direct paths to higher ground.

The Bible on Praise.. **$4**
A beautiful front cover painting by Merlin. Features Merlin's favorite selected verses on praise from thirty-eight books of the Bible.

More Power to You **$9**
Written for people in every day places who need more power in their every day lives.

What's on Your Mind? **$9**
Would you be ashamed for everyone you know to see your thoughts? If so, you urgently need to read and understand *What's on Your Mind?*

Let Me Entertain You **$9**
After years of serving the Lord, Merlin was eager to retire. He wanted to rest, relax and enjoy a quiet life, but God had other plans for him.

From Fear to Faith **$9**
God wants to be intimately involved in your life and help you have victory over your problems.

You Can Be Happy Now **$9**
Everyone desires to be happy! This book will help you to understand how much God wants you to be happy.

Secret Sins **$9**
As you read this book you will be especially pleased to learn that God has provided a simple way for many of us to be delivered from our secret sins.

God's Secret Weapon **$9**
How do we find true, lasting happiness? How can we endure suffering and tragedy? The answer is a powerful weapon and is available in this book.

Please enclose $4 for Shipping

ABOUT THE AUTHOR

Merlin R. Carothers books have been translated into 58 languages. A Master Parachutist and Demolition Expert in the 82nd Airborne Division during three major campaigns of World War II. At the conclusion he served as a guard to Gen. Dwight D. Eisenhower. Later, as a Lt. Colonel in the U.S. Army Chaplaincy he served in Europe, Korea, the Dominican Republic, Panama and Vietnam. He is a pilot, lecturer and retired pastor. He has made many appearances on national television and has traveled worldwide to share what he has learned about praise.

Merlin and his wife, Mary, live in San Marcos, California.